Better Homes and Gardens

Carpentry & Trimwork

Meredith® Books
Des Moines, Iowa

Table of Contents

BUILDING YOUR DREAM

Getting to know your home 6
Safety 8
Working to code 8

CARPENTRY TECHNIQUES

Measuring and marking 10
Holding and measuring in place 12
Square, plumb, and level 13
Special marking techniques 16
Cutting with a circular saw 18
Making miter cuts 20
Cutting with a handsaw 22
Making inside and contour cuts 23
Using chisels 25
Using a tablesaw 27
Using a radial arm saw 29
Using a router 30
Drilling 31
Nailing 35
Fastening with screws 37
Fastening with bolts 39
Removing nails and screws 40
Gluing and clamping 42
Caulking and applying adhesive 44
Making simple, strong joints 45
Making a half-lap or dado joint 47
Fastening with dowels 49
Fastening with a biscuit joiner 50
Applying laminate 51
Shaping and planing 53
Sanding 55
Filling and finishing 57

CARPENTRY

Building a wall 60
Building a wall in place 62
Working with metal studs 64
Furring basement walls 66
Laying out and cutting drywall 68
Hanging drywall 70
Taping drywall 72
Roughing in an opening 74

TOOLS AND MATERIALS

Selecting hand tools 76
Basic power tools 79
Specialized power tools 80
Organize your tools 82
Selecting and buying lumber 84
Selecting wood 86
Selecting moldings 90
Selecting sheet goods 92
Handling and storing materials 93
Selecting nails 94
Selecting screws and bolts 95
Selecting hardware 96
Glue and fastener reference 98

CARPENTRY PROJECTS

Building a workbench.........................100

Building shelves.............................102

Hanging shelves and cabinets................104

Building decorative molding shelves.........106

Organizing a bedroom closet 108

Molding ideas...............................110

Installing base molding 111

Installing crown molding....................114

Wall frame ideas............................117

Installing wall frames......................118

Planning for a chair rail...................120

Installing a chair rail.....................121

Solving door problems.......................122

Cutting a door..............................123

Installing door hinges 124

Installing a lockset 125

Installing a deadbolt lock 126

Installing a prehung door 127

Installing a window 128

Planning for new cabinets...................130

Installing base cabinets 132

Installing wall cabinets....................134

Installing ceiling-hung cabinets 136

Countertop ideas 137

Installing a countertop 138

Glossary....................................139

Index.......................................141

Better Homes and Gardens® Carpentry & Trimwork
Editor: Larry Johnston
Copy Chief: Terri Fredrickson
Copy Editor: Kevin Cox
Publishing Operations Manager: Karen Schirm
Senior Editor, Asset and Information Management: Phillip Morgan
Edit and Design Production Coordinator: Mary Lee Gavin
Art and Editorial Sourcing Coordinator: Jackie Swartz
Editorial Assistant: Kaye Chabot
Book Production Managers: Pam Kvitne, Marjorie J. Schenkelberg, Mark Weaver
Imaging Center Operator: Cari Johnson
Contributing Copy Editor: Ira Lacher
Contributing Proofreaders: Mike Maine, Kristin Crosby McCullough, Maureen Patterson
Contributing Technical Proofreader: Barbara L. Klein
Contributing Indexer: Don Glassman
Other Contributors: Janet Anderson

Additional Editorial Contributions from Abramowitz Creative Studios
Publishing Director/Designer: Tim Abramowitz
Designer/Illustrator: Kelly Bailey
Designer: Joel Wires
Photography: Image Studios
    Account Executive: Lisa Egan
    Photographer: Bill Rein
    Assistant: Rick Nadke

Meredith® Books
Editor in Chief: Gregory H. Kayko
Executive Director, Design: Matt Strelecki
Managing Editor: Amy Tincher-Durik
Executive Editor/Group Manager: Benjamin W. Allen
Senior Associate Design Director: Tom Wegner
Marketing Product Manager: Brent Wiersma

Executive Director, Marketing and New Business: Kevin Kacere
Director, Marketing and Publicity: Amy Nichols
Executive Director, Sales: Ken Zagor
Director, Operations: George A. Susral
Director, Production: Douglas M. Johnston
Business Director: Janice Croat

Senior Vice President: Karla Jeffries
Vice President and General Manager: Douglas J. Guendel

Meredith Publishing Group
President: Jack Griffin
Executive Vice President: Doug Olson

Meredith Corporation
Chairman of the Board: William T. Kerr
President and Chief Executive Officer: Stephen M. Lacy

In Memoriam: E.T. Meredith III (1933–2003)

Photography Courtesy of:
Photographers credited may retain copyright © to the listed photographs:

Focal Point Architectural Products, Inc.
www.focalpointap.com
Page 110 - BL

L = Left, R = Right, C = Center, B = Bottom, T = Top

All of us at Meredith® Books are dedicated to providing you with the information and ideas you need to enhance your home and garden. We welcome your comments and suggestions. Write to us at:
Meredith Books
Home Improvement Books Department
1716 Locust St.
Des Moines, IA 50309–3023

Note to the Readers: Due to differing conditions, tools, and individual skills, Meredith Corporation assumes no responsibility for any damages, injuries suffered, or losses incurred as a result of following the information published in this book. Before beginning any project, review the instructions carefully, and if any doubts or questions remain, consult local experts or authorities. Because codes and regulations vary greatly, you always should check with authorities to ensure that your project complies with all applicable local codes and regulations. Always read and observe all of the safety precautions provided by manufacturers of any tools, equipment, or supplies, and follow all accepted safety procedures.

BUILDING
YOUR DREAM

Getting to know your home

When you plan a carpentry project or go to a building supply center for materials, it helps to know the common terms describing the parts of your house. Some of these terms vary from region to region, but most are understood throughout the country. Although this book deals primarily with interior carpentry projects, it is helpful to visualize how your house is put together. Even a task as simple as attaching a wall shelf or installing baseboard molding requires some knowledge of framing.

The house on these pages combines the elements of old and new construction—a situation you may find in your own home. The two-story section of the house illustrates construction methods and materials common from 1910 to 1960. The one-story addition shows materials and techniques contractors commonly used today.

Framing is the skeleton or basic structure that supports your house. Vertical **wall stud**s run from floor to ceiling. They're usually made of 2×4s, but sometimes 2×6s or even 2×8s are used to allow space for more **insulation**. The horizontal pieces at the tops and bottoms of the walls are called **plates.** The bottom plate rests on a concrete block or formed concrete **foundation**. **Fire blocking** may run horizontally about halfway up walls.

Wherever there is an opening for a door or a window, a correctly sized **header**, made of a single piece of lumber or two pieces of 2× lumber, must span the gap in the framing. For more details about interior framing, see pages 60–65.

Roofs are supported by **rafters** or **trusses**, which use small-dimensioned lumber joined in such a way as to give them strength. **Collar ties** brace the rafters. The roof typically is made of plywood or boards covered with

roofing felt and **shingles**. Eaves are trimmed with **fascia boards**. **Vents** draw hot air from the attic.

Joists made of 2×6 to 2×12 lumber support **subfloors, flooring**, and interior load-bearing walls. The undersides of joists provide nailing surfaces for ceilings.

On the exterior walls the framing is covered with at least three layers of material. First comes **sheathing**, which in older homes is made of 1× lumber often run diagonally. Some sheathing milled with an overlapping joint is called shiplap. Plywood, oriented-strand board (OSB), fiberboard, or rigid foam is used in newer homes. Next comes a paperlike layer to improve insulation and reduce the effects of condensation. Older homes use **roofing felt** (also called tar paper) or reddish-colored building paper; newer homes have **house wrap**, often made of polyethylene. Finally the house is clad in **siding**. This house has horizontal **beveled siding**, but vertical siding and sheet siding also are common. Inside the exterior walls, older homes often have gray-color rock wool (asbestos) insulation; fiberglass is used now.

Interior wall surfaces of older homes usually are covered with **lath**: thin pieces of rough, 3/8-inch thick wood run horizontally. The lath is covered with two or three layers of **plaster**. Today **drywall** is nailed or screwed to the framing, and the joints and nail holes are covered with joint compound. Plastering is a specialized skill that takes years to master, but most homeowners can apply and finish drywall themselves (see pages 70–73).

Gaps around windows (**double-hung sash, casement, fixed-pane, or full-round**), doors, and along walls are covered with **molding**. See pages 110–116 for installing moldings.

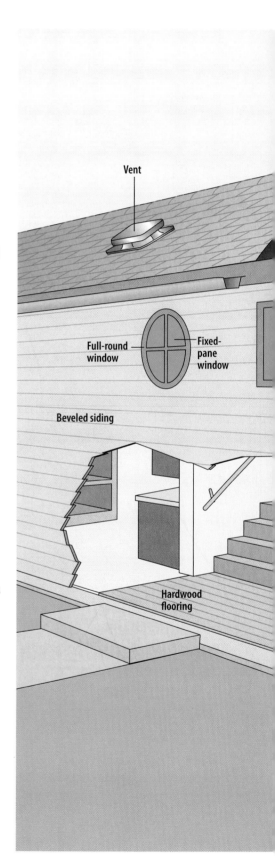

Vent

Full-round window

Fixed-pane window

Beveled siding

Hardwood flooring

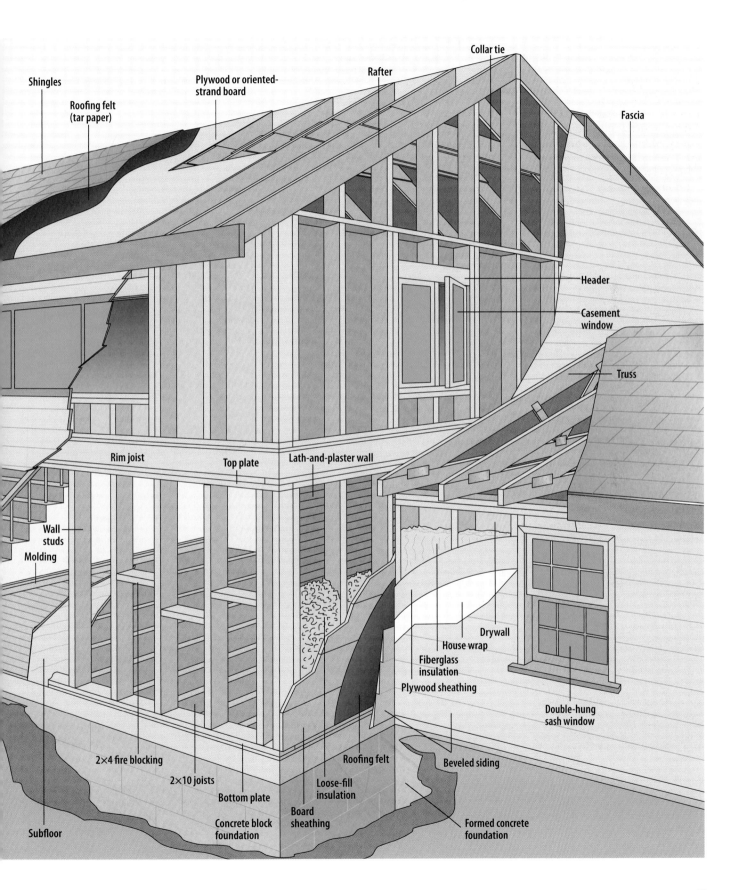

Shingles

Roofing felt (tar paper)

Plywood or oriented-strand board

Rafter

Collar tie

Fascia

Header

Casement window

Truss

Rim joist

Top plate

Lath-and-plaster wall

Wall studs

Molding

Drywall

House wrap

Fiberglass insulation

Plywood sheathing

Double-hung sash window

2×4 fire blocking

2×10 joists

Bottom plate

Roofing felt

Beveled siding

Loose-fill insulation

Board sheathing

Subfloor

Concrete block foundation

Formed concrete foundation

Safety

Tool safety tips

For safety, it is important to follow guidelines and exercise common sense. There are many ways to hurt yourself when working with building materials and tools. Just one moment's lapse of attention can lead to an injury. To minimize risks, keep the following safety tips in mind:

- Use tools only for the jobs they were designed to do. If a tool comes with an instruction manual, take the time to read it to find out what the tool will and will not do.

- Make sure the tool is in good condition before using it. A dull cutting edge or a loose-fitting hammerhead, for example, spells trouble. Also inspect the cord of a power tool to be sure it's not damaged.
- Don't work with tools if you're tired or in a hurry.
- Don't work with tools if you have recently been drinking alcohol.
- Wear goggles whenever the operation you are performing could result in eye injury.

- The safety mechanisms on power tools are there for your protection. Don't tamper with or remove them.
- Avoid wearing loose-fitting clothes or dangling jewelry while you are using tools.
- Keep other people, especially children, at a safe distance while you're using any tool. Before you let children use a tool, instruct them on how to operate it and supervise them as they work.
- Before servicing or adjusting a power tool, unplug it and allow moving parts to stop.

Working to code

Although you may be an amateur working on your own house, you have the same responsibilities to building authorities as a professional carpenter or contractor. Any structure you build must be solid and long-lasting, plumb and square, and constructed of materials appropriate for the job. You must use only those techniques and materials that meet local building codes.

The procedures in this book satisfy most local codes, but be aware that codes can vary widely. Always check with your city or county building department if you are considering adding to or changing the structure of your house in any substantial way or if you think your existing structures might be substandard.

Building codes may seem bothersome, but they are designed to make your home safe and sturdy. Ignoring codes can lead to costly mistakes, health hazards, and even difficulties in selling your house in the future. Minor repairs do not require

permits. Changes involving framing; major projects, such as kitchen or bath remodeling or adding a new room; or jobs affecting plumbing and electrical systems typically do require permits. If you are in doubt, check with your building department before proceeding. Neglecting to do so could lead to the expense and trouble of tearing out and redoing work.

In the course of completing carpentry work, you may expose wiring and pipes. If so, take time to make sure these systems are safe and up to code before you cover them up again.

You never know what kind of building inspector you will encounter when you apply for your permit or during a site inspection: Some can be helpful, friendly, and flexible; others are rigid and unyielding, focusing on the smallest details. No matter what kind of inspector you deal with, your work will go better if you follow these guidelines:

- To avoid unnecessary questions about your plans, seek as much

information as possible and incorporate that information into your plan before you take it in for approval. Your building department may have literature explaining requirements for the type of project you have planned.
- Go to your building department with a plan to be approved or amended; don't expect the inspectors to plan the job for you. Present your plan with neatly drawn diagrams and a complete list of the materials you will be using.
- Understand clearly at what stages of your project you need to have inspections. Do not cover up plumbing or electrical installations that require inspection by finishing walls or floors before the inspector arrives, for instance.
- Be courteous. Take time to do high-quality work. Inspectors often are wary of homeowners because so many do shoddy work. Show the inspector you are serious about doing things correctly.

CARPENTRY
TECHNIQUES

Measuring and marking

Accurate measuring and marking are essential to successful carpentry. A mistake in measuring often means wasted time and material. Though it may seem simple, good measuring technique takes practice.

Don't rush your measuring. Take your time and double-check your work. Heed the old carpenters' maxim: "Measure twice, cut once."

No matter what measuring device you use, become familiar with it and learn how to read it accurately.

Once you've made a measurement, don't trust your memory. Jot down the figure on a piece of paper or a wood scrap.

The best practice is to use the same device for all measurements whenever possible. For example, a poor fit could result if you measure the width of a window for a piece of molding with a yardstick, then measure the molding itself with a tape measure.

Marking the measurement often introduces error too. Make a clear mark (see page 11) using a sharp No. 2 pencil, the thin edge of a sharpened carpenter's pencil, a knife, or a scratch awl.

COMPARE MEASURING DEVICES

Different measuring tapes or rulers can differ slightly, and the discrepancies show up when dealing with long spans of lumber. This can become a problem if you are calling out measurements for someone else to cut. Before you accuse your partner of sloppy cutting, compare measuring devices to be sure they read the same.

For the first few inches, most tapes show ¹/₃₂-inch marks.

Hook slides to compensate for its thickness.

Measure with a steel tape

A steel tape is the most popular measuring device because it's handy and easy to use for most jobs. The hook at the end of the tape slides back and forth slightly to compensate for its own thickness. This means that whether you hook the tape on a board edge for an outside measurement or push it against a surface for an inside measurement, the result will be accurate. The first few inches of most tapes are divided into ¹/₃₂-inch increments, but you will usually work in ¹/₁₆-inch increments.

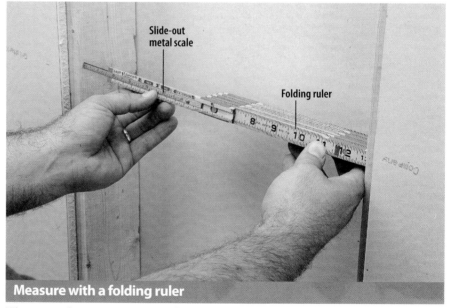

Slide-out metal scale

Folding ruler

Measure with a folding ruler

Where outside measurement is difficult (here the drywall is in the way of measuring between the outside edges of the 2×4s), make an inside-to-inside measurement. A folding ruler with a slide-out metal scale works well for this. Extend it, measure, and hold the slide with your thumb until the measurement is transferred. You can use a tape measure for these measurements, but it is difficult to measure accurately because you have to add an amount to compensate for the length of the tape body.

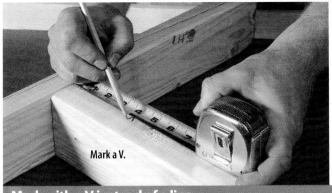

Mark a V.

Slide the square to the mark.

Mark with a V instead of a line

Marking with a simple line often leads to inaccuracies. By the time you're ready to saw, it's easy to forget which end of the line marks the spot—or where to cut on a thick line from a blunt pencil. For greater accuracy, mark your measurements with a V so you know precisely where to strike the cutline. To ensure pinpoint accuracy, place the point of your pencil at the V, slide the square to it, then make your line.

If you need to extend cutlines across several boards, use a framing square. For longer lines—on sheet goods, for instance—use a drywall square.

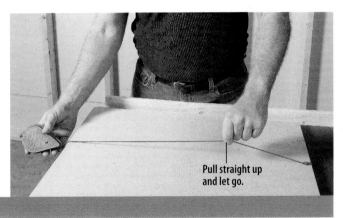

Pull straight up and let go.

Mark for rip cuts

Need to mark a rip-cutline parallel to the edge of a board or a piece of plywood? If precision isn't critical, use your tape measure as a scribing device. Hold your tape so that a pencil laid against its end will trace a line at the correct point. Hold the tape and pencil firmly and pull evenly toward you, letting the tape body or your thumbnail slide along the board edge. For greater accuracy or when you are cutting sheet goods far from the edge, first mark the cutting points at both ends, then snap a chalkline between the two marks. You also can draw the line between the marks using a straightedge and pencil.

Cutline

Scrap

Mark a double line to allow for saw kerf.

Allow for the saw kerf

When you cut material, the saw blade removes some of it as sawdust. When measuring, you must allow for the wood removed by the blade—called the kerf— which is usually about $1/8$ inch wide. If you're making just one cut, mark the waste side of the cutoff line with an X, then make your cut on the waste side. This avoids confusion as to where you should make your cut.

If you are cutting multiple pieces out of the same piece of lumber, make double marks to allow for the kerf.

Holding and measuring in place

- **TIME:** Less than 1 minute for most measurements
- **SKILLS:** A steady hand, a good eye for accurate marking
- **TOOLS:** Pencil, speed square

The most accurate and mistakeproof way of measuring is to not use a measuring device. Simply hold a piece where it needs to fit and mark it. You can do this for a simple cutoff. When you need to cut a board in two directions, use a combination of techniques: Hold and mark, then measure. This method isn't feasible where access is limited or when the lumber being cut is too bulky to be held in place. Take advantage of this foolproof approach when you can.

NO-MISTAKE MEASURING

Carpenters make measuring mistakes every day, so don't be surprised when you do. Here are some common mistakes and how to avoid them:

- Sawing on the wrong side of the line. If you cut on the good rather than the scrap side of the line, the board will be about 1/8 inch short. Always draw an X on the scrap side (see page 11).
- Misreading upside-down numbers. Is it a 6 or a 9? Make sure you know.
- Simply forgetting. Write down all measurements immediately so you won't forget.

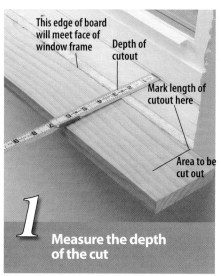

This edge of board will meet face of window frame — Depth of cutout — Mark length of cutout here — Area to be cut out

1 Measure the depth of the cut

When you need to cut a board in two or more directions to make it fit around something, hold the board in position to mark the cutout. Make a mark showing the length of the cutout. Then measure how deep the cutout must be: Measure the distance between the leading edge of the board and the surface it will meet once it's cut.

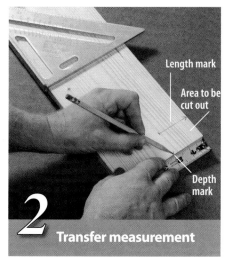

Length mark — Area to be cut out — Depth mark

2 Transfer measurement

Use a square to extend the length mark. With a tape measure, transfer the depth measurement to two places on the board—at the length mark and at the end of the board. With a straightedge, mark a line between the two depth marks. Cut out the corner.

Hold this end out as far as possible—it should just barely touch the measuring point.

Hold and mark for a cutoff

When you need to cut a board to length, begin by checking one end of the board for square. Press the square-cut end against one side of the opening and mark the other end for cutting. To avoid distorting the measurement, don't push the square-cut end into the space any more than needed.

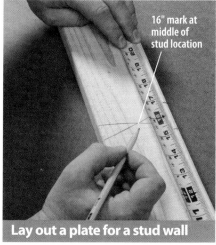

16" mark at middle of stud location

Lay out a plate for a stud wall

Wall studs (the upright 2×4s) are spaced 16 inches on center so 48- or 96-inch-long drywall or paneling will meet at the middle of a stud. To lay out studs, mark every 16 inches from the end of the plate for the center of each stud. Mark 3/4 inch to each side of each center. Draw lines at those marks and draw an X between them to show each stud location (see page 60).

Square, plumb, and level

- **TIME:** 2 minutes or less to check that work is square, plumb, or level
- **SKILLS:** Using squares and levels
- **TOOLS:** Combination, speed, and framing squares; 2- or 4-foot level; other levels

All carpentry projects—from making simple shelves to building walls—require square cuts to make sturdy joints. Check for square at every stage of your work: measuring, cutting, and assembling.

Making sure that work is plumb and level is equally important. Walls, cabinets, doors—nearly every permanent installation—must be plumb (perpendicular to the earth) and level (parallel to the horizon).

It isn't safe to assume any existing wall or floor is square, level, or plumb. Most often it isn't because of imperfect construction or settling that has taken place over the years. Techniques shown in this section will help you keep your carpentry projects straight and true.

Check board ends for square

All your careful measuring will be wasted if you start with a piece of lumber that is not square—one edge will be longer than the other. Check the board end by holding a combination square with the body or handle firmly against a factory edge. If the end isn't square, mark a square line and trim the board.

Use a combination square

With this tool you can easily check for either 45- or 90-degree angles. Also, by sliding the blade, you can check depths. This tool can go out of square if it is dropped, so check it once in a while against a square factory edge (such as the corner of a sheet of plywood).

Inside measure

Outside measure

Blade

Tongue

Use a framing square

For larger jobs, use a framing square. Lay the square up against two members where they meet. If the tongue and the blade of the square rest neatly against the members, the sides are square. Or place the square on the outside. Again, if the square touches the members at all points, the unit is square. When using a framing square for measuring, be sure to read the correct scale—inside or outside.

THREE SIDES MAKE A DANDY SQUARE

Along with a hammer, almost every carpenter's tool belt holds a triangular layout square (shown on page 78). Often called a speed square (the trade name of the original version), it makes marking 45- and 90-degree cutting lines a breeze. Other angles are marked on the body of the square and can be drawn with a fair degree of accuracy. In addition, the three-sided square can be a guide for cutting with a circular saw (see page 19).

Square, plumb, and level *(continued)*

Use the 3-4-5 method

For large projects, test whether a corner is square by using geometry. You don't need to remember the Pythagorean theorem, just remember "3-4-5." On one side, mark a point 3 feet from the corner. On the other side, mark a point 4 feet from the corner. If the distance between the two marks is exactly 5 feet, the corner is square. For larger projects, use multiples such as 6-8-10 or 9-12-15 for greater accuracy.

As a double check, measure the length of the diagonals. If the project is square, the distance between two opposite corners (marked A in the photograph above) will equal the distance between the other two corners (B).

Check for plumb

To see if a piece is plumb (perfectly vertical), hold a level against one face of the vertical surface and look at the bubble in the level's lower glass vial. If it rests between the two guide marks, the piece is plumb.

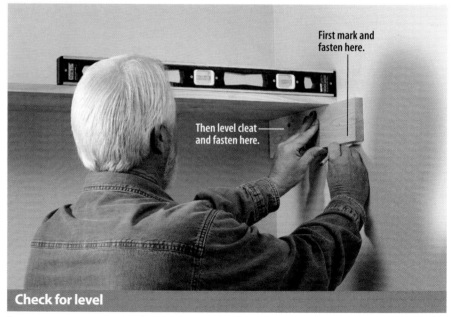

First mark and fasten here.

Then level cleat and fasten here.

Check for level

In most cases, you can simply set your carpenter's level on a piece to see if it's level. Raise or lower the piece until the bubble rests between the lines. Mark the position of the piece and remove the level. (You don't want to risk knocking it to the floor.) Add a fastener to the cleat near the level mark, level the cleat, and finish fastening. Make sure the board is straight, not bowed, where you place the level.

Test for level over long distances with a water level or a board

A water level enables you to quickly check for level in awkward situations or over long distances. Basically a long hose and two transparent tubes filled with water, this tool works on the principle that water seeks its own level. Mark at the water level in both tubes.

If you need to check that a floor is level, select a long, straight board. (Sight down its length to see that it's not bowed.)

Place a carpenter's level in the center of the board and raise one end or the other until the bubble is centered between the two lines. Slide the board around until you are sure you have found the high point of the floor. Level the board from this point and measure the distance from the floor to the bottom of the raised end of the board to see how far out of level the floor is.

Laser accuracy

A laser level casts a bright level or vertical guideline on a surface. Some models hang on a wall by suction; most can mount on a tripod. All are easy-to-use and precise.

TEST YOUR LEVEL

Test a new level for accuracy before buying it. If the first one you try isn't accurate, the next one on the shelf may be. If you own a level, test it to see if it has been knocked out of alignment.

To make sure your level is accurate, set it on a shelf or table and note the location of the bubble. Then turn the level around end for end on the same surface. It should give exactly the same reading.

If it is not accurate, you may be able to adjust it by loosening the four small screws holding the bubble assembly and turning the assembly until it is correct. If the level isn't adjustable, buy a new one.

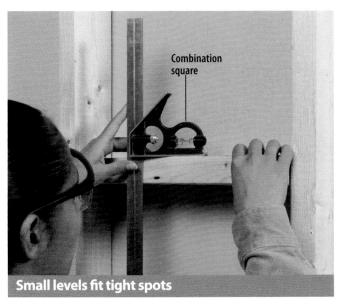

Combination square

Small levels fit tight spots

Where you can't fit a carpenter's level, use a torpedo level (a short version of a carpenter's level) or the level on a combination square. If you are sure that an adjoining framing member or wall is plumb, check that the piece is square to it.

Shim

Plumb a cabinet

When installing cabinets, make sure they are plumb in both directions, or the doors will open or close by themselves. With the cabinet fastened loosely to the wall, hold a level against a vertical framing piece. Tap in shims until the bubble indicates that the cabinet is plumb.

Special marking techniques

A flexible steel tape measure, a square, and a level are usually all you need to mark your lumber for cutting. But sometimes you'll have to mark around the irregular contours of molding, brick, or stone; mark curved shapes; or mark for angles other than 45 and 90 degrees. The techniques on these two pages will help you mark unusual contours.

MAKING AND USING TEMPLATES

When a project part requires multiple cuts or complicated contours, make a template or pattern before you cut the lumber. Often the piece you are replacing can serve as the template. Carefully remove the old piece, take out any nails or screws, place it over the new lumber, and trace its outline.

In other cases you may need to make a template. Cut a piece of stiff cardboard with a knife or make a pattern out of a piece of scrap wood. Cut and trim the template until it fits exactly. This saves experimenting on and possibly wasting your final, expensive materials.

When you trace the template onto your lumber, be sure it does not slide around; you may need to tape, clamp, or tack it in place. Keep your pencil point tight against the template when you trace the part onto the lumber.

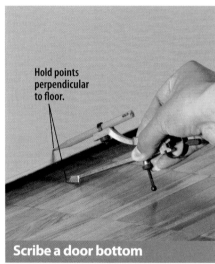

Hold points perpendicular to floor.

Scribe a door bottom

If the bottom of a door is sticking, close it as far as possible. Set a compass to the correct height above the floor—usually the thickness of the threshold plus 1/8 inch for clearance. Hold the compass point against the floor and the pencil end of the compass on the door. Move the compass along the floor, scribing a cutoff line on the door.

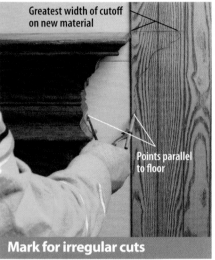

Greatest width of cutoff on new material

Points parallel to floor

Mark for irregular cuts

For a complicated contour cut, use a compass that can be tightened firmly so it won't collapse or expand as you trace the contour. Place the new material next to the object it will fit around. Set the compass to the greatest width to be cut off. Take care to hold the two compass points on the same plane (in this case, parallel to the floor) as you make the mark.

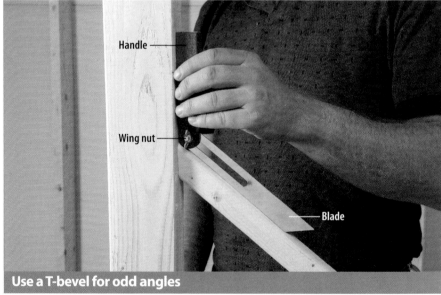

Handle

Wing nut

Blade

Use a T-bevel for odd angles

To duplicate an angle that is neither 45 nor 90 degrees, use a sliding T-bevel. Loosen the wing nut so you can move the blade without difficulty. Hold the handle against one edge and move the blade until it rests against the other edge. Tighten the wing nut firmly. The tool holds the angle you need, allowing you to transfer it to the wood you are cutting. You can use the bevel gauge for inside angles, as shown above, or outside angles. Extend the blade fully for accurate outside readings.

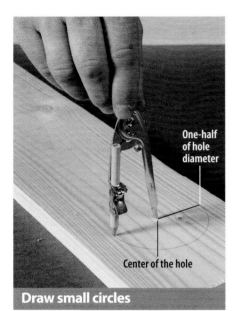

One-half of hole diameter

Center of the hole

Draw small circles

To mark small circles—to make cutouts for pipes or lighting fixtures, for instance—a simple compass will do the job. Mark the center of the hole and set the compass opening to one-half the diameter of the hole. For accuracy, be sure the compass is tightly clamped in position and hold it as perpendicularly to the surface as possible.

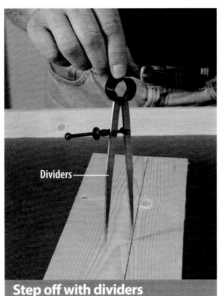

Dividers

Step off with dividers

To mark a series of equidistant points along a straight line, use dividers. Steel points at the base of each leg grip the surface of the material you're measuring for good control. Use a swiveling motion as you step from one leg to the other leg.

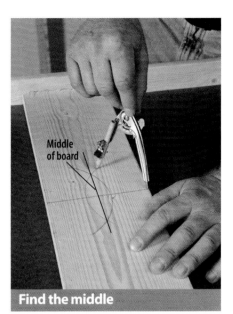

Middle of board

Find the middle

To find the middle of a board, draw a line squarely across the board. Open your compass to a bit more than half the board's width and make two arcing marks at the ends of the line, as shown. Draw a straight line between the points where the curved lines intersect; this is the middle of the board.

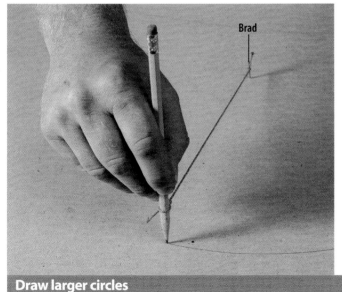

Brad

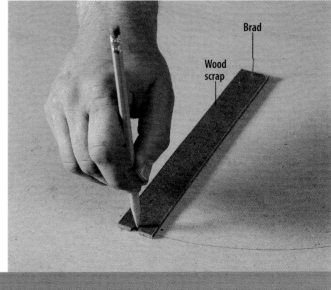

Brad

Wood scrap

Draw larger circles

A compass works well for small circles. If you have to cut out for a sink or another large round object, make your own compass out of a pencil, brad, and string. Be sure to hold the pencil vertically as you draw.

For greater accuracy, make a notch at one end of a small piece of wood. Nail the wood piece into place with a brad at the center

of the circle. Hold the pencil point in the notch to draw a smooth, accurate circle.

Sometimes you may be able to find a round household object, such as a can, a bucket, or a wastebasket, that is close enough to the correct size. Place it on the work and trace around it.

Cutting with a circular saw

You will do a lot of cutting with a circular saw on most projects. Whether crosscutting 1× stock, ripping plywood, or cutting moldings to rough length, you'll do the job better if you follow a few basic rules when using this versatile tool.

Allow the saw to reach full operating speed before you start the cut, then slowly push the blade into the wood. Some carpenters look at the blade as they cut; others rely on the sight notch. Choose the method that suits you best. Avoid making correction turns as you cut. Instead find the right path and push the saw through the material smoothly. It will take some practice before you can do this consistently. This is a powerful tool with sharp teeth, so take care and pay attention whenever you use it.

CHOOSING A CIRCULAR SAW AND BLADES

Choose a circular saw that is comfortable to use. It should be sturdy but not so heavy that it is difficult to handle. You should be able to see the blade and sighting notch in the baseplate easily. Check for ease of depth and angle adjustments. (For more tips, see page 79.)

If you buy only one blade for a circular saw, choose a carbide-tipped combination blade that has at least 24 teeth. It works well for rough work and makes cuts clean enough for most finish work. For fine work buy a plywood blade or a hollow-ground planer blade. For extensive remodeling jobs, get a second carbide-tipped blade that you can use when you may need to cut through nails or other rough materials.

Support the material

Well-supported work results in clean, safe cuts. If the scrap piece is short, support the board on the nonscrap side. If the scrap is long, it could bind the blade or splinter as it falls away at the end of the cut. To achieve a neat cut and avoid saw kickback, support the lumber in four places. Even with such precautions, you may want to make two cuts: one to cut the work roughly to size, the other for the finish cut.

CAUTION

AVOIDING AND PREPARING FOR KICKBACK

Even the most experienced carpenter experiences kickback when a circular saw's blade binds, causing the saw to jump backward. Kickback is dangerous to you and can mar the lumber you are working on. Often poorly supported work—especially a sheet of plywood—is the culprit, but not the only one.

A dull blade will bind and cause the saw to kick. Change your blade or have it sharpened if you have to push hard to make it cut or the wood smells like it is burning.

Warped or twisted lumber will grab a blade. Occasionally certain types of wood grain will grab the blade and cause kickback too. There's nothing you can do about this except be prepared.

Kickback also can occur when you pull the saw backward while cutting or when you try to make a turn. If your cut is going off course, stop the saw, back up, and start cutting again.

For safety, don't wear long, loose sleeves and don't put your face near the saw when you are cutting.

Square the blade

To square a blade, unplug the saw, hold a square against the blade and the base, and adjust the blade. (Be sure to position the square between teeth.) To test whether your blade is square to the baseplate, crosscut a piece of 2× lumber. Flip one piece over and press the cut ends together. If you see a gap at the top or the bottom, the blade is not square.

Align the blade with the cutline

Once you have drawn an accurate cutoff line and have properly supported the board, position the saw blade on the scrap side of the line. The teeth on most circular saw blades are offset in an alternating pattern, half to the left and half to the right. When clamping a guide, align a tooth that points toward the cutoff line.

SET THE BLADE DEPTH CORRECTLY

Before you make any cut, set the blade to cut about ¼ inch deeper than the thickness of the wood. (Be sure to unplug the saw before you do this.) This may seem time-consuming, especially if you are constantly switching between 1× and 2× lumber, but here's why it is worth the trouble:

A circular saw makes a cleaner cut if the saw blade extends only slightly below the bottom face of the material. The good face of the material should face down when you are cutting.

The deeper the blade is set, the more prone it is to binding and kickback, jeopardizing the work and your safety.

Use a square as a guide

With practice, you can learn to cut accurately without using a guide. But use one for cuts that have to be precise. For 90-degree cuts, a speed square works well because it's easy to hold stable. Align the blade, then slide the square into position against the saw's baseplate. Grab the board along with the square so the square stays in position.

Use other guides for angle cuts

You can improvise a saw guide that is as accurate as a miter box. Set a T-bevel to the desired angle (see page 16) and transfer the angle to the board. Select a straight piece of 1× and clamp it parallel to the cutline as a saw guide. To offset the guide correctly, measure the distance between the blade and the edge of the saw's baseplate, and clamp the guide that distance from the cutline.

It may take some experimenting before you get this correct. Be sure to align the blade on the correct side of the line. You can use the same principle for long rip cuts. Clamp a straightedge—the factory edge of a 1× works well—onto the material, setting it back from the cutline far enough to allow for the width of the saw's baseplate.

Support sheet goods

Use a guide

Blade guard lever

Make a plunge cut

For a smoother cut, cut sheet goods with a carbide-tipped combination blade or a plywood-cutting blade. Support the sheet well or the blade will bind. You can do this by setting four 2× support pieces on the floor, a table, or a pair of sawhorses. Arrange two support pieces on either side of the cutline so that when the cut is complete, both pieces of the sheet are stable. Cut with the good face of the material down.

Use a guide to make a long straight cut. The straightedge should be at least as long as the material you are cutting. A straight 1×4 or the factory edge of a piece of plywood works. Measure the distance from the edge of the saw's baseplate to the blade, and clamp the guide that distance from the cutline. Set the saw into place, and check alignment with the cutline. Clamp the opposite end of the guide the same distance from the edge.

A plunge cut, also called a pocket cut, starts a cut in the middle of a board or sheet. Set the blade to the correct depth. Retract the safety guard and tilt the saw forward, setting the front of the baseplate on your work. Start the saw and lower it slowly into the cutline until the base rests on the stock. Complete the cut.

Because you expose the blade, any twist could result in dangerous kickback. Be careful.

Making miter cuts

A miter joint is made when two pieces of wood are angle-cut or bevel-cut at the same angle, then joined to form a corner. Most often, two pieces that have been cut at 45 degrees are joined to make a 90-degree corner. Miter cuts must be precise. If they are off even 1 degree, the corner will be noticeably out of true.

The most inexpensive way to make angle or bevel cuts in narrow stock is to use a miter box—a jig for holding the saw at the proper angle to the work. If you have numerous miter cuts to make, consider buying a power mitersaw (see the opposite page).

Lay a scrap of 1×4 or some other suitable material into the miter box before you use it. This allows you to saw completely through the work without marring the bottom of the miter box. Place the workpiece against the far side of the miter box, positioned as it will be when in use, and make the cut with a backsaw. Hold the work firmly against the back of the box with your free hand.

When using a miter box, correctly measuring and marking for the cut are more critical than the cutting technique. Whenever possible, make the miter cut first, then cut the other end of the piece to the proper length with a straight cut.

Miter box is a saw guide

Essentially, a miter box is a jig holding a saw at the proper angle.

Power saw saves time

If you have a number of cuts to make, consider renting or buying a power mitersaw. A sliding compound mitersaw offers the most versatility.

Scale shows miter angle

The scale on the front of the mitersaw is calibrated. The center setting is 0 degrees, allowing you to make a 90-degree cut. The numbers increase on the left and right, allowing cuts of other angles. The most common cut settings for trimwork are the 0- and 45-degree settings.

Install blade on arbor

Before operating, unplug the saw and make sure the blade is properly set. Mount the blade on the arbor. Tighten the blade bolt with the wrench provided by the manufacturer. The blade teeth point down and back toward the fence.

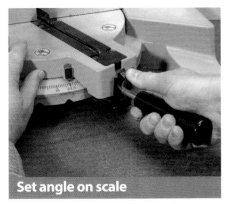

Set angle on scale

To set the angle, unlock the handle and move the table to the desired setting. The manual for your saw shows how to lock and unlock the table handle.

Lock setting for cut

Once the saw is at the desired cut setting, lock the saw table in place.

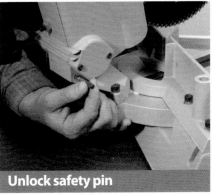

Unlock safety pin

A mitersaw has a pin to lock the head down for transportation and storage. The saw's manual shows where it is and how to release it to operate the saw.

OPERATE SAFELY

Mitersaws can be dangerous if used improperly. Follow these steps to ensure safe operation:

- Read the manufacturer's manual carefully. Make sure you fully understand the instructions before attempting to operate the saw. If you are unsure of yourself, ask the salesperson or rental agent to demonstrate proper usage.
- Wear safety glasses or a face shield for protection from flying wood chips.
- If the work produces excess dust, wear a dust mask.
- Power saws are noisy. Wear proper hearing protection.
- Keep guards in place and in proper working order. Don't operate a saw without a guard.
- Wait for the motor to reach full speed before you start the cut.
- Release the trigger after making the cut and let the saw blade stop before you raise the saw head.

LASER ACCURACY

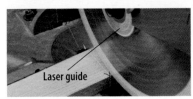

Laser guide

A laser guide, available from home centers, casts a line that makes it easy to align the outside of the saw blade with a mark on the workpiece. It turns on automatically when the saw starts.

Cutting with a handsaw

Although power tools make accurate cutting simple, sometimes a handsaw is more convenient. Learn the proper technique, and hand-cutting may turn out to be easier than you expected.

Make a crosscut with a handsaw

To crosscut narrow stock, set the blade's heel (nearest the handle) at a 45-degree angle to the work. Set the teeth on the scrap side of the cutline. To keep the blade from wandering, use your thumbnail as a guide until the saw starts cutting.
Pull the saw back toward you several times to start the cut. Don't force the blade; let the weight of the saw start the cut while you guide it. Saw with a rocking motion, starting the downstroke with the saw at a steep angle to the wood, flattening the angle as you make the stroke.

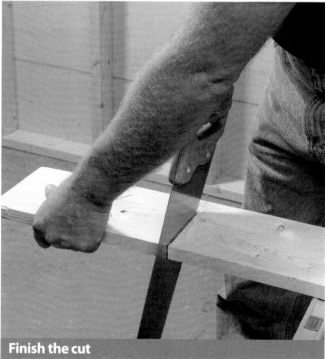

Finish the cut

When you near the end of the cut, support the scrap end of the piece of wood. Grasp it firmly with your free hand, exerting a slight upward pressure to keep it from binding. This also keeps the piece from snapping off and splintering on the last stroke.

Make a cutout

To notch the corner of a board, position the blade of the saw so it is perpendicular to the work as you near the end of each cut. That way, the bottom of the board is cut the same distance as the top. Often it is helpful to reverse the position of the saw, as shown above.

Making inside and contour cuts

Often you need to make a cut in the center of a part or make a curved or irregularly shaped cut. These cuts require two basic steps: drilling or plunge-cutting an access hole into the material, then making the curved cut with a narrow-bladed tool that can follow the contour.

To begin an inside cut, make a plunge cut with a circular saw (see page 20) or a jigsaw (shown at right). Finish the cut with a jigsaw (sometimes called a saber saw). If you find it difficult to make a precise plunge cut, drill a ¼-inch starting hole for the jigsaw blade. (Some blades may require a larger hole.) Drill the hole in the waste area rather than right on the cutting line—especially if the finished work will be visible.

Do not attempt to make a curved cut with a circular saw. Doing so not only can damage your saw and saw blades but can also cause dangerous kickback.

Make an inside cut

How you start an inside cut depends on the material you're cutting. With lumber and sheet goods, the safest way is to drill a starter hole at each corner of the cutout, as close as possible to the cutlines. Insert the blade of a jigsaw or keyhole saw into one of the holes and complete the cut.

If you are experienced with a jigsaw, make a plunge cut. Tip the saw forward on its baseplate, as shown above. Start the saw and slowly lower the blade into the wood along the cutline. The blade tends to dance before cutting into the surface, which can badly mar your work. You may want to practice on a scrap of wood first.

Cut holes into drywall

For a clean cut, score the paper face of the drywall with a knife before sawing it. Poke the tip of a drywall saw (a type of keyhole saw) into the drywall at a cutline. Either push or punch the saw handle with the heel of your hand.

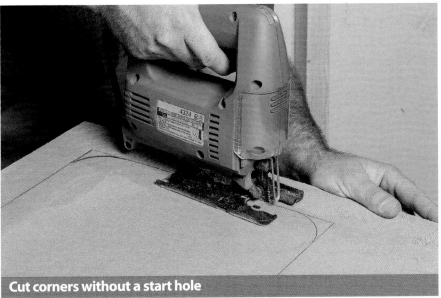

Cut corners without a start hole

You can maneuver a jigsaw around fairly tight corners, but not 90-degree turns. Use a three-step procedure to cut such corners. On your first approach to a corner, cut just up to the intersecting line. Carefully back the saw up about 2 inches and cut a gentle curve over to the next cutline. Continue in this direction, supporting the scrap material as you cut, until the scrap piece is free. Then go back and finish trimming the corners with short, straight cuts from both sides of the corner.

Making inside and contour cuts *(continued)*

Cut curves with a jigsaw

Make most curved cuts with a jigsaw. Once you get the knack of using this tool, you can cut curves that are as smooth as any line you can draw. Be sure the piece you are going to cut is stable; clamp it if necessary and make sure the blade path is clear beneath it.

Start the saw and begin the cut. Guide the saw slowly, without forcing the blade. Turning too sharply can break a blade. If the saw begins to bog down or overheat, you're trying to cut too fast. If you wander from the line, don't try to make a correction with a sharp turn. Instead steer gently back to the line or back up and start again. Support the scrap material as you reach the end of each cut to prevent it from breaking off.

Use a coping saw for fine work

A coping saw is ideal for intricate cutting. This hand tool allows you to set the blade in any direction in relation to its frame. To begin a cut from the inside of a board, remove the blade from the saw frame and reinstall it through a starter hole. For delicate cuts, install the blade with the straight faces of the teeth toward the handle so the saw cuts on the backstroke. A scrollsaw is a power saw for similar work.

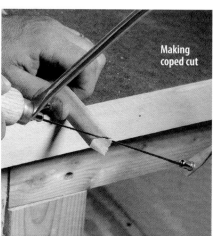

Making coped cut

Coped end — End cut at 90°

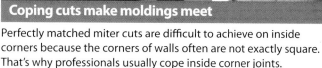

Coping cuts make moldings meet

Perfectly matched miter cuts are difficult to achieve on inside corners because the corners of walls often are not exactly square. That's why professionals usually cope inside corner joints.

Start by cutting the first piece of molding at a 90-degree angle so it butts against the adjacent wall. To cope the overlapping piece, make an inside 45-degree miter cut, as shown in the left photo above. Use a coping saw to cut away the excess wood along the molding profile. Backcut slightly (cut a little more off the back of the piece than the front) to ensure a neat fit. Whenever possible, make the coped cut first, hold the piece in place, then mark for the straight or miter cut on the other end.

Using chisels

Although you may not use a chisel every day, nothing can replace one for making mortises, dadoes, or notches. If you buy just two sizes, get ¼- and ¾-inch chisels. An old one often comes in handy for demolition jobs.

Whenever you pick up a chisel, keep both hands behind the cutting edge of the blade. As you work, point the chisel away from your body. Because it takes two hands to operate a chisel, always clamp or anchor your material. Save yourself wasted effort and ruined materials by keeping your chisels sharp. A properly sharpened chisel should slice through paper easily.

Drive wood-handle chisels only with a wood mallet; a metal hammer quickly mushrooms the handle end. Chisels made to be driven with a hammer usually have plastic handles.

1 To sharpen with a whetstone, grind the cutting edge

A dull chisel edge looks flat and reflects light. It also may have nicks in it. Drip a pool of oil onto a whetstone. Brace the whetstone firmly on a flat surface. Hold the chisel, beveled face down, at an angle slightly steeper than the bevel so you are not grinding the entire beveled face. Press the blade gently and slide it along the stone.

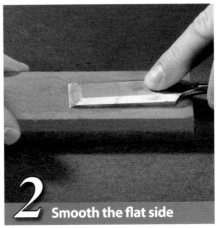

2 Smooth the flat side

Turn the chisel over and lay its flat side on the whetstone. Add more oil if the stone is dry or if a thick paste has built up. Hone the flat side by pressing gently, moving the chisel with a circular motion. You don't want to grind a new cutting edge onto this side; remove only the burrs created after grinding the beveled face.

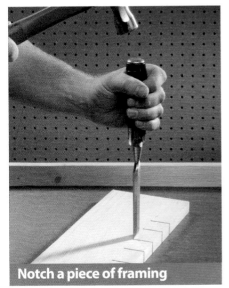

Notch a piece of framing

Set your circular saw blade to the desired depth of the notch and make cuts at the top and bottom of the notch. If the notch is wide, make one or more cuts in the center of the notch as well. Position the chisel with the bevel facing outward. Begin cutting at a slight outward angle that gets flatter as you proceed.

Make a deep mortise cut

It is difficult to chisel deeply into a narrow board without splintering it. Begin by drilling a series of adjacent holes within the scored outline of the mortise. If possible, use a drill bit that is the same diameter as the width of the mortise. Finish the cut with a chisel, holding the beveled face toward the inside of the mortise as you gently tap.

SHARPENING NICKED OR BADLY WORN TOOLS

To sharpen a nicked or badly worn chisel, a single-cut file or a bench grinder works better than a whetstone.

To sharpen a chisel with a file, clamp the chisel tightly in a vise with the cutting edge pointing up. Remove nicks by filing nearly perpendicularly to the chisel edge. Then hold the file at the same angle as the chisel bevel and file diagonally across the bevel. Work slowly and evenly to obtain a sharp edge. Remove burrs on the flat side with an oiled whetstone.

To remove nicks from a chisel's blade with a bench grinder, hold the chisel nearly perpendicularly to the wheel and grind until the nicks disappear. Regrind the bevel, using the guide on the grinder to hold the chisel at the bevel angle. Go slowly: Never let the cutting edge blacken or get red hot.

Using chisels *(continued)*

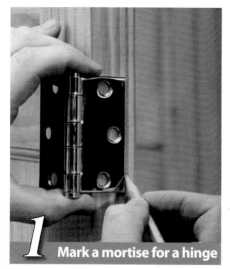

1 Mark a mortise for a hinge

Do not attempt to lay out a hinge mortise just by measuring; use the hinge itself as a template. Position it correctly on the edge of the door and mark its perimeter with a sharp pencil. Mark for the depth of the mortise on the face of the door.

2 Score the lines

To prevent the wood grain from splintering at the edges of chisel cuts, score the lines you just marked by gently cutting with a utility knife. Once you have established the score lines, go over them again with the knife until you have cut to the depth of the mortise.

3 Chisel the mortise

Hold the chisel with the beveled face down at the angle shown. Whenever possible, cut in the direction in which the wood grain runs. Otherwise, the chisel follows the grain deeper into the board than you intended. Drive the chisel to the depth of the mortise, making several slices across its width.

Making dadoes

1 Lay out a dado

When laying out a dado (a groove across the grain of a board), take care to draw straight, square lines that mark the exact thickness of the part that fits into the dado. Use a square to mark both the top and bottom edges of the dado.

2 Cut lines with a circular saw

Adjust your circular saw blade to the dado depth—one-third or one-half of the wood thickness ($1/4$ or $3/8$ inch for $3/4$-inch boards). Clamp a guide to the board to cut the two outside lines squarely. After cutting the two outside lines for wide dadoes, make a series of passes through the middle of the dado.

3 Chisel out the waste

Using a chisel the same width as or narrower than your dado, tap out the remaining slivers of wood. Start from one edge and work toward the middle, then work from the other edge. Smooth the bottom of the notch by scraping it with your chisel, flat side down.

Using a tablesaw

A tablesaw is the principal tool in most woodworking shops. Look for one that is accurate and powerful enough to handle 2× material. A small, lightweight tablesaw is handy if you need to move it around often. However, the smaller table area makes it more difficult to use and you will have a hard time making accurate cuts on large pieces such as a sheet of plywood.

The fence of a tablesaw should move smoothly along its guide rails and lock firmly and parallel to the blade.

If possible, turn the saw on and watch the blade. There should be no hint of a wobble. A belt-driven tablesaw works more smoothly and lasts longer than one with direct drive.

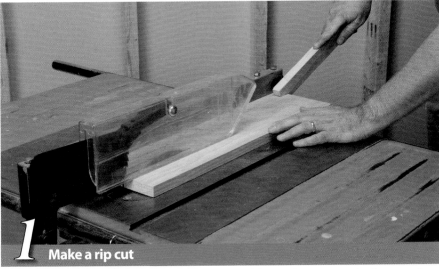

1 Make a rip cut

Set the fence parallel to the blade and check it by measuring the space between the blade and the fence at the front and the rear of the blade. Set the blade height ¼ inch above the top of the board. Start the motor and allow it to reach full speed.

Hold the lumber against the fence so the wood glides smoothly and rides against it as you push it forward. Keep your fingers at least 6 inches away from the blade; use a push stick when you come to the end of the cut (see page 28).

2 Make a crosscut

For a square cut, make sure the miter gauge is perpendicular to the blade; slip it into its channel and square it using the edge of the table as a guide. Set the blade height ¼ inch above the board and start the motor. Hold the board firmly against the miter gauge and slide the wood toward the blade. Hold the board only at the miter gauge. If you hold the wood on both sides of the cut, the blade may bind, causing dangerous kickback. Keep your fingers well away from the blade.

TABLESAW, RADIAL ARM SAW, OR POWER MITERSAW?

A tablesaw and a power mitersaw are an ideal combination. The tablesaw allows you to make long, straight cuts with ease. A tablesaw also is superior for cutting dadoes. A power mitersaw can crosscut long, narrow pieces easily—a difficult task with a tablesaw.

A radial arm saw does the jobs of a tablesaw and power mitersaw, but not quite as well. It crosscuts with less precision than a mitersaw. Making long rip cuts and cutting sheet goods are difficult. Cutting angles other than 90 degrees may be cumbersome too.

CAUTION

SAFETY MEASURES FOR A TABLESAW

Because a tablesaw runs so smoothly, it's easy to let safety consciousness lapse while working with one. But inattention or careless use of a tablesaw can injure anyone, whether a beginner or an experienced user.

Always keep your fingers well away from the blade. Never wear long sleeves or loose clothing while using a tablesaw. Never reach across the saw blade while it is running. Keep push sticks and an antikickback feather board handy and develop the habit of using them (see page 28). Turn off the saw and let the blade stop when you need to free a piece of wood that has become stuck.

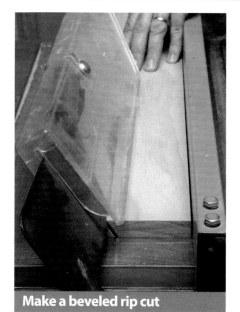

Make a beveled rip cut

To set the bevel, use an adjustable bevel gauge, or mark the bevel angle on the end of the board and tilt the blade until it aligns with the mark. Hold the board against the blade at the correct location, slide the fence against the board, and lock the fence in place. Follow the same procedures as for a rip cut (see page 27).

Adjust the blade height

Before every cut, adjust the blade height so it is about ¼ inch above the top of the board you are cutting. This makes a cleaner cut and helps avoid binding and dangerous kickback. If you are cutting a sheet of plywood that is warped, you may need to raise the blade higher so it cuts through the sheet completely at all points. Always unplug the tablesaw before making blade adjustments.

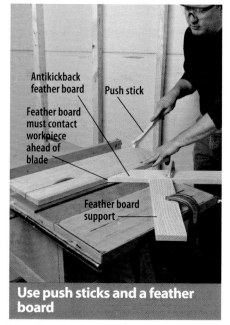

Antikickback feather board
Push stick
Feather board must contact workpiece ahead of blade
Feather board support

Use push sticks and a feather board

To make a feather board, cut one end of a 16-inch-long 1×6 at 60 degrees, then cut 8-inch-long kerfs ¼ inch apart into the angled end. When clamped as shown above, it holds stock against the fence and prevents kickback in case the blade binds. Push sticks keep your hands well clear of the blade; make them out of 1× lumber or ½-inch plywood, or buy commercial ones.

Dado or groove

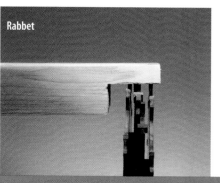

Rabbet

Tenon made with an adjustable dado blade

Cut dadoes, rabbets, and tenons

With a dado blade, you can cut a variety of groove sizes. With a regular dado blade, sandwich a combination of chippers between the two outside cutter blades to set the desired width. Set the blade height above the table to cut to the desired depth. Mark the depth on the board and hold it next to the blade as you adjust it. Adjustable dado blades dial to the desired width.

If you need to make a groove wider than the dado blade, make repeated passes, moving the board a little less than the width of the blade for each pass.

On a tablesaw, you will not be able to see the cut as you make it, so test your settings on a scrap piece to make sure the dado is the correct width and depth. Then cut the project part.

Using a radial arm saw

A radial arm saw works best for crosscutting wood, but you can use it for ripping as well, as long as you take it slowly and use precautions (see below right). With attachments available on some models, you can use a radial arm saw as a router or a sander.

A radial arm saw table is made of particleboard or plywood rather than metal because the saw blade must cut into the table slightly to cut boards completely. When the tabletop becomes shredded after years of use, you should replace it. The fence, usually a piece of 1×2, needs to be replaced more often.

A sliding compound mitersaw can make some of the same cuts as a radial arm saw, but it is designed for two purposes only: miter-cutting and crosscutting boards. A power mitersaw is more portable than a radial arm saw and can be set up easily on sawhorses for cutting moldings at a site.

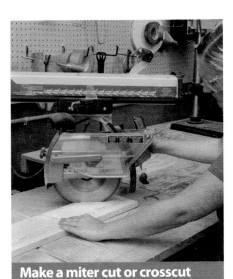

Make a miter cut or crosscut

Test your saw for accuracy by cutting scraps at 45 and 90 degrees and adjust the fence or saw if necessary. To make the cut, hold the board firmly against the fence. Make sure the board is fully supported and lies flat on the table. Pull the saw toward you, cutting the board so the saw kerf is on the scrap side of the line.

Cut a dado or rabbet

To cut a notch for a dado or rabbet, raise the blade to the desired height; test the cut depth on a scrap. Check that the board lies flat; any warp will distort the cut. Cut on each side of the notch, then make a series of cuts in the interior. Clean out the notch with a chisel. If you have many notches to cut, use dado blades.

Make a rip cut or beveled rip cut

Turn the saw so the blade rotates up against the board, the opposite of a crosscut or dado cut. Start the saw with the blade slightly raised above the tabletop, then lower it to the cutline. To avoid kickback, hold the board firmly as you feed it into the blade. Pull the board through the blade to finish the cut.

Cut molding with a power mitersaw

A power mitersaw is convenient for cutting molding. Hold the piece firmly against the fence, start the saw, and lower the blade to make the cut (see page 21). Often the cut will begin at the middle of a molding; make your marks accordingly. Hold crown molding at the correct angle for cutting with triangular blocks.

CAUTION

RADIAL ARM SAW SAFETY

Radial arm saws can be extremely dangerous. Not only can you cut yourself with the blades, but the saw almost certainly will kick a board back at bulletlike speed if you are not careful. Develop these safety habits:

- Never remove the saw guard. Take the time to adjust the guard for maximum safety before making each cut.
- When ripping boards with a radial arm saw, use a push stick and feather board like those for a tablesaw (see page 28). Also stand to the side of the board so if it shoots back, it won't hit you.
- Keep work flat and well supported so the blade will not bind.

Using a router

With the versatility and power of a router, you can form profiles on board edges and machine various grooves in board faces. In addition to choosing from several bits (shown at right), you can set your bit to the depth of cut that suits you. Often, it's possible to save money by milling your own lumber rather than buying expensive moldings.

For rounding off edges, a router produces a far more professional-looking finish than a rasp or sander.

 Chamfer
 Core box
 Corner round
 Dado
 Dovetail

 Flush trim
 Plunge cut
 Rabbet
 Straight bit
 V-groove

CHOOSING A ROUTER

As a general rule, the more power a router has, the cleaner and faster it will cut. A variable-speed router has some advantages because some bits work better at lower speeds.

Buy a router that can be attached to a table easily or has a variety of guides you can assemble quickly. This will save plenty of work time when setting up the router.

Be sure you can change bits and adjust the router depth easily.

Choose among many bits

Piloted bits, such as the flush trim, rabbet, chamfer, and corner round, are self-guiding; they pilot on the edge of the board so you don't need to use a guide or template when cutting with them. Use these bits to shape edges of boards or to trim laminates after they have been applied. Bits with ball-bearing guides usually work more smoothly.

Other bits require a guide or template. You can use two or more bits in succession to make intricate shapes.

CAUTION

BITS ARE SHARP

Most of the time, you will not even see your router bit as you work. Don't let that lull you into complacency: A router's sharp bit, rotating at tremendous speed, can do major damage in a millisecond. Keep your hands well away from the work.

Use a guide

You can make accurate cuts using a router guide. Sometimes a simple straightedge suffices; just hold the baseplate tightly against it as you cut. A guide like the one shown above allows you to follow a precut template. A router table, which holds the router upside down with the bit protruding through the tabletop, offers greatest accuracy and ease of use for many router tasks.

Use specialty guides

Numerous guides are available for special purposes. To cut smooth circles or curves, use a trammel guide like the one shown above. A router bit spins clockwise, so you get the best results if you move the router counterclockwise. You can buy guides and jigs for cutting dovetail joints, box joints, hinge mortises, and more.

Drilling

Some carpenters still haul out a brace and auger bit to bore a hole, but for most, the electric drill is the tool of choice. With a variable-speed power drill, you can drill a hole of about any size, buff and grind, and even mix paint or mortar. With a drill/driver, you can drive screws into wood or metal.

Some carpenters keep two drills on hand—one for drilling pilot holes, the other for driving screws. That way they don't waste time changing bits. A power drill with a keyless chuck speeds up a change of bit, although you may find that bits slip during heavy-duty tasks.

A drill press is handy for precise drilling. But the techniques here and on the next three pages show how you can bore holes that are straight enough for general carpentry without one.

CHOOSING A DRILL

- Avoid buying a low-quality drill with a ¼-inch chuck. It doesn't have the power you need and soon burns out. One tip-off to a better-quality tool is the cord. Look for a long cord that flexes more like rubber than plastic.
- A hammer drill, or a drill with a hammer option, bangs at the material as it drills. It's useful when drilling in masonry.
- A cordless drill/driver can make your work easier, but only if it is powerful enough to do most things a corded drill can do.
- Different tasks often require different drill speeds, which makes variable speed a useful feature.

You should use a slower speed for a large spade bit than for a ⅜-inch twist drill, for instance.
- For heavy-duty work, choose a corded drill with a ½-inch chuck. This runs at a slower speed but has more power than a standard ⅜-inch drill.
- For additional information on choosing a drill, see page 79.
- Some tools that look like drills are actually screwdrivers. The most common are designed for driving drywall screws. These set the head of the screw at the required depth—deep enough to make an indentation but not so deep that it damages the drywall.

Choose the correct bit

Some of the more common drill bits are shown at right. Auger bits, either solid-center or expandable, often have a tapered square shank end for use with a hand brace. The augers shown have shanks to fit a drill chuck. Twist drills are commonly available in fractional sizes from ¹⁄₁₆ to ½ inch and drill wood, metal, and plastics. A brad-point bit makes a cleaner hole in wood than a twist drill. For holes from ½ to 1¼ inches in diameter, use a spade bit. For making holes in masonry or concrete, use a carbide-tipped masonry bit. A countersink bit bores a shallow hole so you can set screw heads flush with or below the surface. A combination bit drills both a pilot hole and a countersink hole in one step. For holes larger than 1¼ inches or for drilling precise holes through tough materials, use a holesaw. Drill/drivers take screwdriver bits of various styles.

The star drill and awl, while not used with a drill, are handy for special situations. Drive the star drill with a hammer to make holes in masonry and concrete. The awl is handy for marking hole centers for drilling. You also can poke holes with one to start small screws in soft wood.

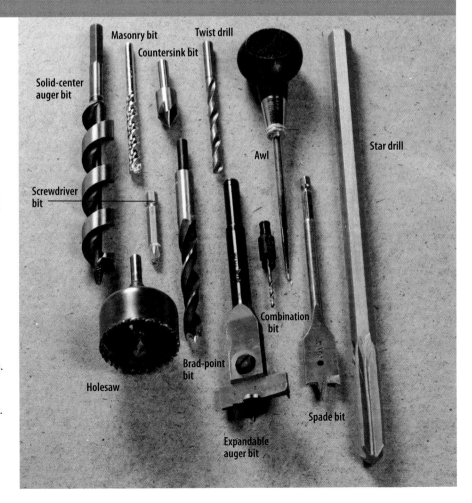

Masonry bit
Twist drill
Countersink bit
Solid-center auger bit
Awl
Star drill
Screwdriver bit
Combination bit
Brad-point bit
Holesaw
Spade bit
Expandable auger bit

Drilling *(continued)*

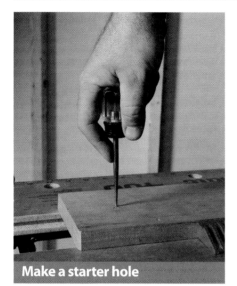

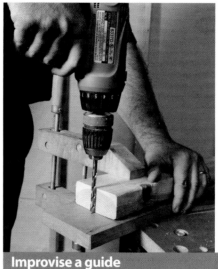

Make a starter hole

A bit tends to skate off the mark when you begin boring a hole, so make a shallow starter hole with an awl or a center punch. In soft woods, a gentle tap on an awl with the palm of your hand does the job. On hard woods or metal, tap the center punch or awl with a hammer.

Improvise a guide

Usually you'll want to drill holes that are perpendicular to the board. Check that the bit is square as it enters the material by clamping a piece of square-cut scrap lumber in place, as shown above. With some drills, you can hold a square on the material and against the body of the drill. When you need to drill a hole at an angle,

fashion a guide by cutting the edge of a piece of scrap lumber to the desired angle. Clamp the guide so it aligns the tip of the bit exactly on your center mark. Begin the hole by drilling perpendicularly to the surface. Once you have gone deep enough to keep the bit from skating away, shift the drill to the angle.

CAUTION

AVOID DAMAGING YOUR DRILL BITS AND DRILL

Drilling is a simple procedure, but it's easy to dull or break a drill bit. Be careful not to overheat the bit; an overheated bit becomes dull quickly. If you see smoke, stop drilling immediately. Pause occasionally and test the bit for heat by quickly tapping it with your finger.

Unlike a professional model, a homeowner-type drill is not designed for constant use. If you feel the body of the drill heating up, stop and give it a rest or you could burn it out.

Hold the drill firmly as you work. If you tilt or twist the tool while drilling, the bit might break, especially a small twist drill.

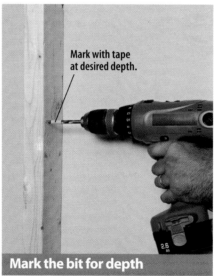

Mark with tape at desired depth.

Mark the bit for depth

To drill one or more holes to the same depth, wrap masking or electrical tape around your drill bit so the bottom edge of the tape contacts the surface of the material at the desired hole depth. Drill with gentle pressure. Back the bit out as soon as the tape touches the surface of the material.

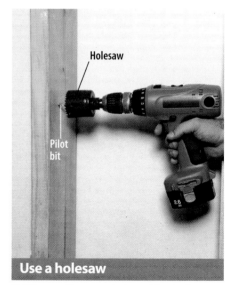

Holesaw

Pilot bit

Use a holesaw

Drill large-diameter holes with a holesaw. Make a center mark for the pilot bit. If the material you are drilling isn't supported on the back, prevent splintering when the bit penetrates it by clamping a piece of scrap stock against the back. Or drill until the pilot bit pokes through, then drill from the other side.

Drill until point of spade bit barely pierces material.

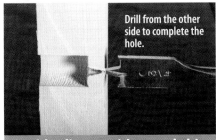
Drill from the other side to complete the hole.

Avoid splinters with a spade bit

When using a spade bit, drill through the material until the tip of the bit begins to poke out the back side of the material. Carefully reverse the bit out of the hole. Complete the hole by drilling from the other side, using the pilot hole you've just made.

Back up to pull wood particles out.

Keep particles from clogging hole

When you drill deep holes into thick material with a twist drill, wood particles build up in the flutes of the bit, causing it to bind. Don't force the bit in farther than it can go or you will burn it out. Instead feed the bit into the wood slowly and back out of the hole frequently while the drill motor is running. This pulls trapped wood

Clean particles from the flute.

particles to the surface. If you're working with sappy or wet wood, shavings may clog the flute of the bit. If this happens, stop the drill and use the tip of a nail to scrape out the shavings. If the bit jams, reverse the drill rotation. Pull the bit straight out.

1. Drill pilot hole. See page 98 for pilot hole sizes.

3. Countersink for screw head.

For the best fit, drill three holes ...

When you use standard wood screws to fasten parts together, drill pilot and shank holes to provide clearance for the screw to ensure easy driving and avoid splits. Using a bit that is slightly smaller than the screw, drill through the top and bottom piece. Then select a bit that is as thick as

2. Drill for screw shank. See page 98 for shank hole sizes.

4. Insert the screw.

the screw shank and drill through the top board. The screw should slide easily through this top hole and grip tightly as it passes into the smaller hole. Use a countersink bit to bore a space for the screw head. When you drive the screw, it fits without cracking the wood.

For flush screw heads, drill to this point.
For counterbored screw heads, drill to this point.

or use a combination bit

If you're driving a number of screws, buy a combination countersink-counterbore bit, which drills three holes in one action. Be sure to get the correct bits for the screws you are driving. If you want the screw head to be flush with the surface, drill until the spot marked on the bit, above, is even with the surface. To counterbore the screw head, drill deeper.

Drilling (continued)

DRILLING THROUGH METAL

A high-quality twist drill with titanium nitride (TiN) coating works best for drilling metal. But if you work slowly, you can drill metal with any sharp twist drill. The trick is to keep the bit and the metal lubricated with light oil at all times. If the bit is dry even briefly while drilling, it can overheat and become dull.

Before you start, drip motor oil onto the bit and the spot to be drilled. Take your time, adding oil as you work and stopping often to keep the twist drill from overheating.

If you need to drill a hole larger than ¼ inch in diameter, drill a smaller hole first, then follow with the bigger bit.

Drill into masonry and concrete

Use a carbide-tipped masonry bit to drill into brick or concrete surfaces. Brick is usually easy to drill into, while concrete is more difficult. Check the bit often to make sure it's not overheating.

A trick that helps is to spray the bit and the hole with window cleaner as you work. This keeps the bit cool, and the foaming action of the cleaner brings debris up and out of the hole.

When drilling into concrete, you occasionally will run into an especially hard spot (usually a rock embedded in the concrete). Pull the bit out, insert a masonry nail or thin cold chisel, and bang with a hammer to crack the rock and give your bit a place to grab. If you have much masonry drilling to do, buy a hammer drill, which hammers the bit as you drill.

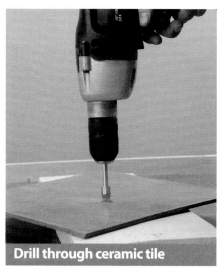

Drill through ceramic tile

Wall tiles are usually soft, but floor tiles can be tough. Nick the surface of the tile just enough so the bit doesn't wander as you drill. Keep the bit and the hole lubricated with a few drops of oil. Use a masonry bit or a special tile bit like the one shown above.

Bit with lead screw

Expandable bit for brace

Use a brace and expandable bit

A brace is an old-fashioned tool that works faster than you may expect. To drill large-diameter holes, bore until the lead screw of the bit pokes through the material. Then drill through from the other side. To get more pressure on the brace, hold its head against your body and lean into the work.

Plug-cutting bit

Bore and plug for a finished look

For a handcrafted appearance, drill pilot holes, then drill a wooden plug using a plug-cutting bit. Drive the screw in, squirt a little white glue into the hole, and tap in the plug. Allow the plug to stick out slightly. After the glue has dried, chisel and sand the plug flush with the surface.

Nailing

The quickest way to make a job look shoddy and amateurish is to make a nailing mistake that mars the wood. All your careful measuring and cutting will be for naught if the wood ends up with "smiles" and "frowns" made by a hammer that missed the nail, or if you bend a nail while driving it.

Professional carpenters make nailing look easy. When properly done, pounding a nail home is a series of smooth, fluid motions. You may never be as fast at nailing as a professional carpenter who gets plenty of practice, but you can learn to drive nails without damaging the material or yourself.

GETTING THE HOLDING POWER YOU NEED

How well a nail holds in wood depends on how much of its surface contacts the wood. The longer and thicker the nail, the better it holds.

When possible, use the Rule of Three: A nail should be three times as long as the thickness of the board being fastened. Two-thirds of the nail then will be in the board you're fastening the first one to. If the nail must penetrate through empty space or drywall, increase the nail length by that distance.

A thick common nail holds better than a thinner box nail, but not if it splits the wood. In that case, most of its holding power is lost. Special nails, such as ringshank and cement-coated nails, hold better than standard nails. A headed nail holds better than a finishing nail, which has a small head.

Nails are sold in penny sizes, abbreviated "d." A six-penny nail is a 6d nail. Penny sizes indicate length:

2d=1 inch	8d=2½ inches
3d=1¼ inches	10d=3 inches
4d=1½ inches	12d=3¼ inches
6d=2 inches	16d=3½ inches

Set the nail

Practice on scrap pieces before you drive nails into finished work. To ensure that the hammer strikes the nail and not your fingers and that the nail is driven into the board squarely, hold the nail vertically and grip the hammer near the end of the handle. Lightly tap the nail until the nail stands by itself.

If you must drive a nail near the end of a board, reduce the risk of splitting the wood by drilling a pilot hole or blunting the nail point. (Turn the nail upside down and tap the point with the hammer.) Another way to prevent splitting is to avoid driving several nails on the same grain line in the wood.

Proper technique makes nailing easy

Once the nail is set in place, remove your hand from it. Keep your eye on the nail as you swing the hammer, letting the weight of the hammerhead do the driving.

Beginners tend to hold a hammer stiffly and keep their shoulders rigid, swinging from the elbow. This leads to a tired, sore arm, and mistakes. Loosen up. Your whole arm should move as you swing from the shoulder. Keep your wrist loose so you can give the hammer a final snap at the end of each blow. The entire motion should be relaxed and smooth.

With the last hammer blow, push the head of the nail flush or nearly flush with the surface of the wood. The convex shape of the hammer face allows you to do this without marring the surface.

Nailing *(continued)*

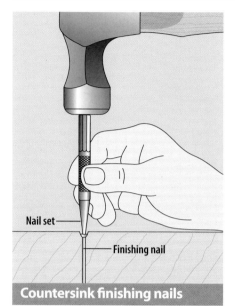

Countersink finishing nails

In most cases, it's best to drive the heads of finishing or casing nails below the surface. You can fill the holes with wood filler later. This takes little time and leads to a much better looking finish than nails driven flush. Hold a nail set against the nailhead and tap the nail in.

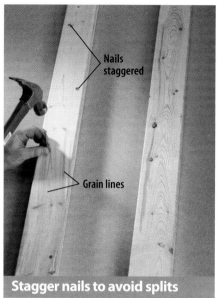

Stagger nails to avoid splits

When driving several nails along the length of a board, stagger them. This avoids driving neighboring nails through the same grain line; two nails are twice as likely to wedge the grain apart and split the board as one nail. If the work will be visible, stagger the nails in a pattern.

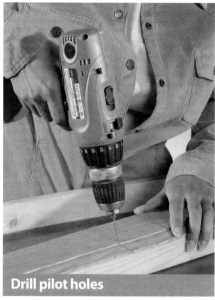

Drill pilot holes

When nailing within 2 inches of the end of a board or into hardwood or moldings, drill pilot holes to avoid splitting the wood. Hole sizes are: 3d, 1/16-inch hole 3/4 inch deep; 4d, 1/16-inch hole 1 inch deep; 6d, 5/64-inch hole 1 5/16 inches deep; 8d, 3/32-inch hole 1 5/8 inches deep; 10d, 7/64-inch hole 2 inches deep; 12d and 16d, 7/64-inch hole 2 1/4 inches deep.

USING MASONRY NAILS

Masonry nails attach materials to concrete, brick, or masonry block. With flat (called "cut" or "square-cut") masonry nails, turn the nail in the direction of the grain so it's less likely to split the wood.

You can use a standard hammer, but the job is easier with a heavy mallet. Hold the board in place and drive the masonry nail through it. Once the nail hits the masonry surface, strike it with hard strokes. With subsequent nails, check to see whether you have dislodged any nails; you may have to drive farther.

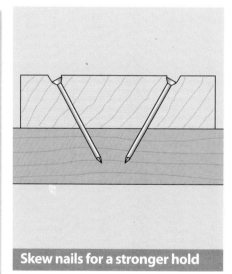

Skew nails for a stronger hold

Where you cannot use as long a nail as you would like, drive nails at an angle. Drive one nail at about a 60-degree angle in one direction, then drive another nail at the same angle in the opposite direction. The skewed nails make it difficult to pull the board loose. Set the nailheads for a finished appearance.

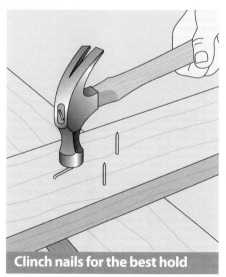

Clinch nails for the best hold

If looks are not as important as strength, use nails about 1 inch longer than the combined thickness of the pieces you're fastening. Drive the nails, then turn the boards over and bend the exposed portion of the nails so they are nearly flush with the surface and parallel to the wood grain. The resulting joint is extremely difficult to pull apart.

Fastening with screws

It's easy to see why screws fasten so well: The threads grip wood fibers in a way a smooth nail cannot. When a screw is driven home, the threads exert tremendous pressure against the screw head to hold the fastener firmly in place. With the right tools (see box, below), driving screws can be almost as quick as nailing. If you make a mistake, it's easy to remove a screw without damaging your work. Screws must be driven with care, however. If you do not start out straight, there is no way to correct the mistake as you continue driving the screw. Without a pilot hole, the screw may split the wood and the screw will not hold securely. If the pilot hole is too large, the screw will not grip well.

TOOLS TO USE

Power-driven screws hold tightly, go in quickly, and are easy to remove. Here are some tools that make working with them even more convenient:

- A variable-speed, reversible drill starts the screws slowly and removes them if necessary.
- With a magnetic sleeve, screws stick to the bit, making it easy to drive them into hard-to-reach places. Changing bit tips is easy: Simply press them into the sleeve.
- Have a collection of screwdriver bits on hand, particularly #1 and #2 phillips bits, as well as some slotted bits.
- Consider buying square-drive screws and bits. These bits fit into and grab the screw slot better than phillips-head and slotted screws.

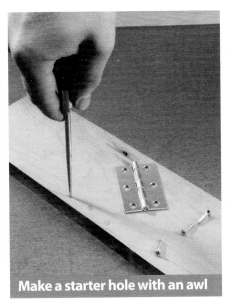

Make a starter hole with an awl

Small hardware screws seldom require pilot holes in softwood (see box, below right). But they do need starter holes. Poke a hole with a scratch awl. Give it a few twists, back it out, and you're ready to drive the screw. Always drill a pilot hole into hardwood such as oak or maple.

Power-driving makes assembly go faster

Driving even a few screws by hand can take a long time, so consider using a drill/driver with a screwdriver bit. When driving slotted screws, take care that the bit does not wander partway out of the slot or you could damage the workpiece surface. Take your time or the bit may slip out of the slot. Maintain firm, even pressure as you work.

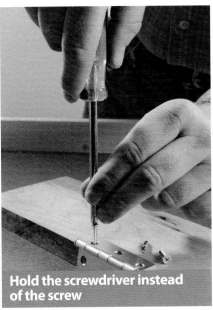

Hold the screwdriver instead of the screw

Start screws by holding the screwdriver handle with one hand and the screwdriver blade with the other. Don't hold the screw. If the screw is spinning around and not going into the wood, place two hands on the handle to apply more pressure.

WHEN DO YOU NEED A PILOT HOLE?

If there is a danger of cracking the wood, drill a pilot hole, no matter how small the screw. For instance, if the wood is brittle or if you are driving a screw near the end of a board, almost any screw can split the wood. But if you are drilling into a sound board at a spot 2 inches or more from its end, it usually is safe to drive a #6 or thinner screw without a pilot hole. If you are drilling into plywood or framing lumber, you should be able to drive #8 screws without pilot holes. You should always drill a pilot hole into hardwood to prevent breaking the screw. For advice on drilling the correct-size hole, see page 98.

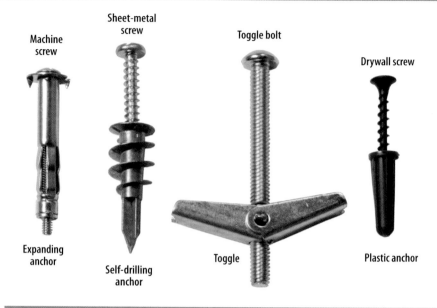

Machine screw

Sheet-metal screw

Toggle bolt

Drywall screw

Expanding anchor

Self-drilling anchor

Toggle

Plastic anchor

Use phillips-head drywall screws

Drywall screws are sold by the pound at reasonable prices, so you can use them in most places you would use nails. If you use a magnetic driver, place the screw onto the bit first, then set the tip of the screw into place on the material. If you need to hold the screw, hold the head only, not the sharp threads. Particleboard screws are handy too; they countersink themselves.

Attach items to walls with special fasteners

The best way to attach brackets and other items to a wall is to drive a screw into a stud. But often that's not possible. The fasteners shown above are designed to hold items firmly in drywall or plaster. To use expanding anchors and plastic anchors, drill holes, and tap the unit into the wall; the anchor spreads and grips as you tighten the screw. Use self-drilling anchors only in drywall. You don't need to drill a hole; just screw the anchor in and insert a screw. To use a toggle bolt, drill a hole large enough for the folded-back toggles to fit through. Push the toggles through the hole and turn the bolt until the toggles are snug up to the back side of the wall. Anchors are rated for the weight they can support.

FASTENING TO METAL WITH SCREWS

For fastening thin sheet metal or soft metal, such as brass, use sheet-metal screws. Drill a hole of the correct size through the pieces and drive in the screw. Some screws are self-drilling; you simply drive the screw and it drills its own hole through the metal.

For heavier metals, drill a pilot hole through the metal; then drive in a self-tapping screw.

For metal $\frac{1}{8}$ inch or thicker and where you want a strong joint, buy a tap and a drill bit of the correct size. The tap cuts machine-screw threads into a hole so you can screw in a machine screw or bolt.

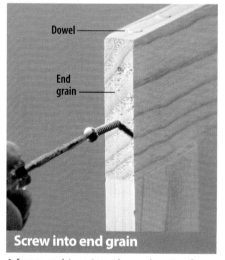

Dowel

End grain

Screw into end grain

A fastener driven into the end grain of a board does not hold as well as one driven into the face or edge. In end grain, use a longer screw than usual. Where holding power is critical, drill a hole and insert a dowel, as shown, into which you can drive the screw.

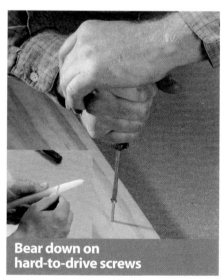

Bear down on hard-to-drive screws

If the going gets tough, exert pressure on the screwdriver with the palm of one hand and turn it with the other. If you still can't drive the screw, remove it and drill a slightly larger pilot hole. Another solution is to lubricate the threads with candle wax and try again.

Fastening with bolts

Nails and screws depend on friction between the fastener and the wood to do their jobs. When you tighten a nut on a bolt, however, you're actually clamping adjoining members together, producing the sturdiest of all joints. All types of bolts require a hole bored through both pieces being joined together. Drill holes for machine screws, as well as bolts and carriage bolts, the same diameter as the screw or bolt shank.

CAUTION

DON'T OVERTIGHTEN

Overtightening bolts can strip threads and damage wood, reducing the holding power of the bolt. Tighten the nut and bolt firmly against the wood, give them another half-turn, then stop.

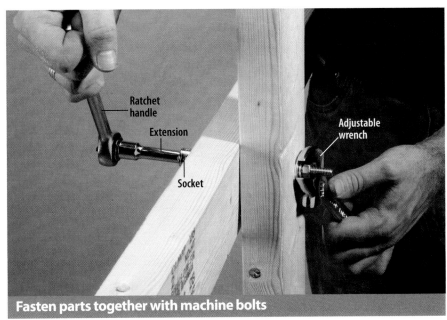

Fasten parts together with machine bolts

A machine bolt has a hexagonal head and a thread running partway or all the way along the shank. When fastening wood together, slip a flat washer onto the bolt and slide the bolt through the holes in the parts. Add another flat washer, then a lock washer. Screw the nut on, and tighten it. The flat washers keep the nut and the bolt head from digging into the wood. The lock washer prevents the nut from coming loose. Use two wrenches to draw the nut onto the bolt: one to steady the nut, the other to turn the bolt head.

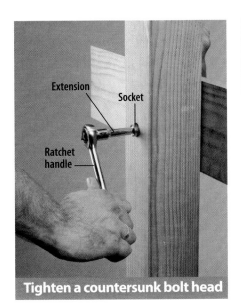

Tighten a countersunk bolt head

To install a machine bolt in a hard-to-get-at place or when you countersink the bolt head, use a socket wrench with a socket extension to reach into the recess. Hold the nut with another wrench.

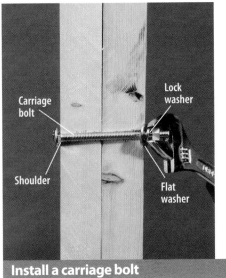

Install a carriage bolt

A carriage bolt has a plain, round head with a square shoulder below it. Insert it into the hole and tap the head flush with the surface. Slip a flat washer, a lock washer, and a nut onto the bolt. Tighten the nut. The square shoulder keeps the bolt from spinning as the nut is tightened.

No washer is needed under the head. The lock washer should keep the nut from working loose. As added protection, thread another nut onto the bolt, snug it against the first, then jam the nuts by turning them in opposite directions, as shown above.

Removing nails and screws

Whether you're correcting mistakes, disassembling an old structure, or recycling used lumber, you'll find it's worth it to learn how to remove fasteners quickly and neatly.

Removing screws often is just a matter of reversing your drill and screwing the old fastener out. You may be faced with a stripped head or an extra-tight screw (see opposite page).

Most commonly, you'll be faced with removing nails. Don't just start whacking away in frustration or you'll damage the wood. Use the methods shown here to remove nails relatively easily and with minimum marring.

Pry with a flat bar

If the head of the nail is not set into the wood, it may be possible to slide a flat bar under it and pry up the nail. Tap the notch of the chisellike head of the bar under the nailhead and pull back on the bar. Because of its smooth, flat body, a pry bar makes only a slight indentation in the board as you remove the nail.

Use a wood block

There are two good reasons for using a wood block when removing a nail with a claw hammer. First the added height gives your hammer extra leverage, making it much easier to pull the nail out. Second, the block protects your work. Without it, the head of the hammer would dig in and make an unsightly indentation.

Pound so claws grab nailhead.

Dig nails out with a cat's paw

A cat's paw removes nails that are embedded deeply into lumber. Its drawback is that it must dig deeply into the wood to grip the nailhead. Place the clawed tip behind the nailhead. Drive the claws under the nailhead, pry the nail partway out, then use a hammer and block or a flat bar.

Tap out to release nails.

Tap in to expose nailheads.

Pound out board to loosen nails

If you can reach the back side of the joined material, strike the joint from behind, then drive the members back together from the front. This usually pops the nailheads out far enough for you to grip them with your hammer claw.

Tight-work hacksaw

Cut nails

Where access is tight, sometimes you can disjoin two members by sawing through the nails. If you have a reciprocating saw with a metal-cutting blade, this is easy. Otherwise use a tight-work hacksaw. After you break the joint, use a nail set to force the heads out, then remove the nails.

Nail set

Putty knife

Punch through and pry

To avoid splitting molding, punch through the finishing nails that hold it in place with a nail set or pin punch. Try not to make the hole larger; use a small-diameter nail set. Pound the head of the finishing nail deeply into the molding. You'll feel the board come loose. Once you have punched the nails through, pry off the molding with a putty knife or chisel, taking care not to mar the wood.

Clean out a painted screw head

When removing old screws that have been painted, take the time to clean the paint out of the slots. If you don't clean the head, you may strip the screw head, making it even more difficult to remove. Place a screwdriver as shown above and tap with a hammer.

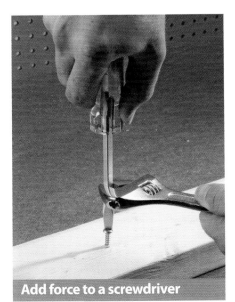

Add force to a screwdriver

If you need greater turning power, use a screwdriver with a square shank and grip the shank with an adjustable wrench. Adjust the wrench so it fits tightly onto the screwdriver. Press down on the handle of the screwdriver with the palm of your hand as you turn with the wrench.

Cut a stubborn nut

Rusty or damaged bolt threads make it hard to remove a nut. You can solve the problem quickly with a hacksaw. Align the saw blade so it rubs against the threads and cut down through the nut. You will cut off about one-third of the nut. Once you have done this, it's easy to knock the nut loose or unscrew it.

REMOVING OLD SCREWS

Here are some tips for removing stubborn screws:

For a slotted screw that has been stripped so much that a screwdriver can't get a good hold, deepen the slot by cutting into it with a hacksaw.

Extremely tight screws often can be loosened with heat. Hold the tip of a soldering gun against the screw head for a minute or two, then try loosening it.

For stripped phillips-head screws, it sometimes helps to drill a small hole into the center of the head to give the screwdriver more to grip.

For an extremely stubborn screw, buy a screw-and-bolt extracting tool. Drill a small hole into the screw head, insert the tool, turn it with a wrench, and twist the screw out.

Gluing and clamping

A joint is stronger if you use glue in addition to nails or screws. For some projects, glue alone is enough.

Read the label before you purchase a bottle of glue. You want the project to be successful, and so does the glue manufacturer. Printed on the label is detailed information about each type of glue. The label states if the glue is appropriate for your project. It also tells you what safety precautions to take when using the glue.

Use contact cement to attach wood veneers or plastic laminates to wood surfaces. Apply the cement to both surfaces and let them dry. Align the parts precisely before you join them—the first bond is permanent (see pages 51–52).

Use paneling adhesives to attach sheet goods to walls. For interior projects, use carpenter's glue with aliphatic resin. This is superior to standard white glue because it sets up faster, resists heat and moisture better, and is stronger. For the glue to work, however, the pieces must be clamped together firmly until the glue sets.

For those times when you wish you had a third hand to hold a workpiece, use a clamp. A clamp helps grip objects while you work on them. It also holds a project tightly together while glue sets.

The amount of time a clamp has to remain in place depends on the type of adhesive, room temperature and humidity, and the complexity of the project. Follow the glue manufacturer's suggestion for clamping. If the manufacturer says to clamp 24 hours, give the glue 24 hours to set. Shorting the time may be disastrous.

CHECK THE EXPIRATION DATE

Glue failure rarely happens, but when it does, one of two things has occurred: Either you used the wrong glue for the job or it has exceeded its shelf life. The shelf life of glue varies. The standard shelf life is one year. Some glues have a shelf life as short as three months. If you have forgotten when you bought a bottle of glue, dispose of it properly and buy a new bottle. Mark the date on it, thus taking the guesswork out of later trying to remember when you bought it.

CLAMPING TIPS

Dry-fit pieces to make sure they align correctly before gluing and clamping.

Use as many clamps as you need to make sure that the glued surfaces remain squeezed together tightly at all points. Wipe off excess glue with a damp rag.

Apply just enough clamping pressure to create a tight bond; don't distort the wood.

Recheck the fit after tightening the clamps and make any necessary adjustments.

Spring clamps grip fast

For light work, these are the easiest clamps to use. Apply glue to both pieces and place them together in correct alignment. Squeeze the clamp handles to spread the jaws. When you release the handles, the springs clamp the work together. You may want to have several sizes of these inexpensive clamps on hand.

These clamps work well for cabinetmaking and other woodworking projects. Because their jaws are made of wood, you need not worry about marring your project—as long as the jaw faces are clean. Adjust a clamp to almost any size or angle simply by turning its two hand screws.

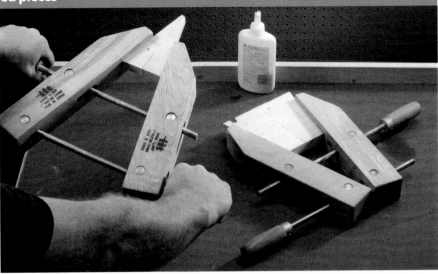

Block to protect wood

C-clamps

Pipe clamps

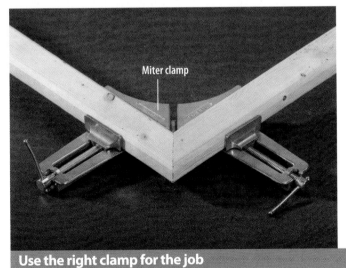

Miter clamp

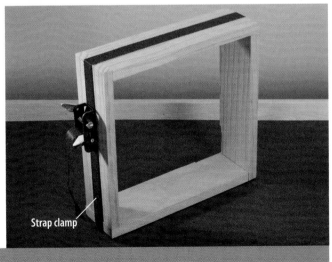

Strap clamp

Use the right clamp for the job

C-clamps are inexpensive and work well when the pieces are not too wide. Use blocks of wood to keep the clamps from marring the boards. Bar clamps and trigger-type quick clamps also are good choices. For miter joints, use miter clamps that hold the boards at a 90-degree angle. For large projects, use pipe clamps. You should alternate them as shown to prevent buckling. A strap clamp works well for cabinetry projects. It clamps several joints at once without marring the wood.

Caulking and applying adhesive

■ **TIME:** About 20 minutes to caulk around a bathtub or countertop, 10 to 30 minutes to adhere laminate or paneling
■ **SKILLS:** Smooth, steady control
■ **TOOLS:** Utility knife, caulking gun, notched trowel

It takes practice to lay down a clean-looking bead of caulk. Practice on scrap materials or start in an inconspicuous area before you caulk an area that is highly visible.

Choose among numerous adhesives that are designed for particular jobs. (See chart, below.) When working with adhesives, be careful to apply

them smoothly and evenly so the piece adheres uniformly. Avoid applying too much adhesive; cleaning up messes can take longer than the initial job.

Apply a bead of caulk

Make sure the joint to be caulked is free of dirt and grease and that no gaps wider than your bead of caulk are present. Snip the nozzle of the caulk tube at about a 45-degree angle. The closer to the tip you cut, the smaller the bead will be. You may need to puncture the inside seal with a long nail. Squeeze the caulking gun handle until caulk starts coming out; move smoothly to apply an even bead.

Attach paneling to walls with adhesive

To attach paneling to walls, apply a bead of adhesive onto either the wall or the back of the panel. Use a notched trowel or make a squiggle pattern using a caulking gun. Press the panel against the wall, then pull it out slightly. Wait a few minutes for the adhesive to get tacky (the manufacturer's instructions tell you how long), then press the panel against the wall again.

Cover large areas with a notched trowel

For a smooth, even application, use a notched trowel to apply adhesives. Check the adhesive container for the type and size of notches the trowel should have. Hold the trowel nearly parallel to the surface to make sure the adhesive sticks. Tilt the trowel up at a 45-degree angle and press firmly to spread the adhesive.

SELECTING ADHESIVES

Adhesive type	Primary use	Holding power	Moisture resistance	Set/cure time	Type of applicator
Contact cement	Applying wood veneer and plastic laminate.	Excellent	Excellent	Must dry first / 1–2 days	Brush, notched trowel, or paint roller
Epoxy adhesive	Bonding almost any materials. Must mix the parts.	Excellent	Good	30 minutes / 1–10 hours	Throwaway brush or flat stick
Panel adhesive	Attaching drywall or paneling to walls.	Good	Fair	1 hour / 24 hours	Caulk tube or notched trowel
Carpenter's glue	Bonding wood together for small projects.	Good	Fair	30 minutes / 24 hours	Squeeze-type container
Cyanoacrylate (superglue)	Bonding small items of almost any material.	Good	Fair	1–2 minutes / 24 hours	Squeeze tube

Making simple, strong joints

■ **TIME:** About 10 to 20 minutes per joint, depending on complexity
■ **SKILLS:** Making square cuts, drilling, using fasteners
■ **TOOLS:** Square, ruler, pencil, saw, drill, drill bits, hammer, nail set, screwdriver

Strong, good-looking wood joints are essential to all carpentry and woodworking projects. Here are some of the simplest and strongest joinery methods. Each of these joints can be made with hand tools, but if you have shop tools, such as a tablesaw or power mitersaw, the job goes faster and the joint is tighter. None requires cabinetmaking expertise.

You'll need to hone your measuring, cutting, and fastening skills to make neat, sturdy joints. See pages 10–43 for a review of the basic techniques.

All of the joints shown on this page are butt joints—two square-cut pieces joined together by positioning the end of one member against the face or edge of another member. The joints can be fastened with nails or screws only. They will be stronger, however, if you reinforce them with metal reinforcements, dowels, a plywood gusset, or a wood block.

Butt joints

Wood block

Corner braces

Plywood gusset

Corrugated fastener with dowels

Flat corner iron

Dowels

Making simple, strong joints (continued)

Lap joints are stronger than butt joints and often look better as well. To make an overlap joint, simply lay one of the members on top of the other and nail or screw it into place. For a full-lap joint, cut a notch into one member that is as deep as the second piece is thick. Glue and clamp the two pieces together, adding fasteners if you prefer. The

half-lap joint is a strong joint (see pages 47–48).

Dado joints are attractive and strong but require careful measuring and cutting for accuracy. A stopped dado has the strength of a dado and hides the dado from view if it is placed at the back (see pages 47–48).

For a corner that hides the end grain, make a miter joint. Cut the pieces at the same angle (usually 45 degrees), then glue the joint and drive finishing nails.

These joints can be fastened with screws or nails and may be reinforced with dowels (see page 49) or biscuits (see page 50).

Lap joints

Overlap

Full-lap

Half-lap

Dado joints

Dado

Stopped dado

Miter joint

Miter

Making a half-lap or dado joint

■ **TIME:** About 1 hour to make two joints
■ **SKILLS:** Precise marking, cutting, chiseling
■ **TOOLS:** Circular saw, tablesaw, or radial arm saw; square; chisel

Shelves and other wooden structures made with half-lap or dado joints are stronger and more attractive than those made with butt joints. Half-laps and dadoes are more refined work, but these strong joints don't require advanced woodworking skills, just basic marking, cutting, and chiseling. Both joints require precise notches. Use sharp saw blades and chisels. To hone your notching skills, practice on scrap lumber.

Dado joints

The term "dado" refers to both the type of joinery and the cut. A dado (DAY-doh) is a channel that runs across the grain of the wood. (A channel parallel with the grain is called a "groove" or a "plow.") For joinery, the depth of a dado is usually one-third or one-half the thickness of the board, and the width equals the thickness of the joining part that seats in the dado. Make a dado with a circular saw and chisel, a tablesaw fitted with a dado blade, or a router (see pages 26, 28, 30). Assemble the parts with fasteners or glue or both. When you set up to cut a dado, make test cuts first with scraps.

Half-lap joints

A half-lap joint is made by removing half the thickness, typically the same thickness for each piece, of the end of each connecting piece. Half-laps form strong corners. You can reinforce the joint with fasteners, but take care not to split or crack the end. When gluing, keep the joint clamped and allow it time to dry thoroughly. You make a half-lap with a tablesaw or a router with a straight bit.

Mark for a dado

Hold the part that seats in the dado against the piece to be dadoed. Mark along both sides with a sharp pencil or a knife or mark one side and use a scrap piece as a spacer to mark the second line.

You also can lay out the dado with a tape measure and square. Cut the dado with a circular saw, tablesaw, or router. Cut a dado into scrap wood first to verify your dimensions and setup.

1 Mark for a half-lap joint

Overlap the pieces to be joined. Mark the half-lap on the first board by running a sharp pencil or a knife along the edge of the board. Mark the depth of the half-lap on the end and edges. Using the same method, lay out the half-lap on the second board or cut the first half-lap; set it over the second board to make the layout.

2 Cut a series of kerfs ...

For a half-lap joint, set your saw blade to cut exactly halfway through the board. Keeping the blade on the inside of the half-lap area, cut the half-lap shoulder or shoulders using a guide for accuracy, then saw a series of kerfs about ⅜ inch apart in the half-lap. You can use a tablesaw or router too (see pages 27 and 30).

or cut out a notch

For a half-lap at the end of the board, simply cut out a notch. Cut the shoulder with a circular saw. Then cut out the half-lap area with a backsaw or Japanese pull saw, starting at the end of the board. To help keep the saw straight, draw guidelines from the end to the shoulder cut on both sides.

DADO JOINTS FOR BOOKSHELVES

- Dado joints are useful when building fixed shelves in bookcases. Before cutting the grooves, carefully measure where you want to position the shelves. Shelves installed with dado joints can't easily be moved if you want to reposition them later. Also measure the thickness of the shelves before cutting the dadoes.
- Before cutting the dadoes, double-check that you have positioned them correctly on the sides of the bookcase so that the shelves are level when installed.

3 Clean out and join

Using a chisel with its beveled surface down, clean the kerfed wood out of the half-lap. Make sure the visible edges are straight and the surface of the half-lap has no bumps. Dry-fit the pieces to make sure they are tight. Apply carpenter's glue, clamp, and fasten with nails or screws.

Fastening with dowels

- **TIME:** 1 hour to make two dowel joints
- **SKILLS:** Drilling
- **TOOLS:** Backsaw, hammer, drill with an extra-long bit

A dowel joint is strong, and you can make one without special tools. Making the joint takes care: You must hold the boards square as you work, you must hold the drill as straight as possible to keep from poking a hole through the edge or side of a board, and the surfaces of joined pieces need to be perfectly flush. Work on a flat surface to keep the face of the boards even. If possible, clamp the boards together before adding the dowels.

Buy a dowel jig if you have many joints to make. Though you can work without one, it makes the process easier. A dowel jig clamps to the edge of the workpiece and acts as a drill guide. This ensures that the drill bit enters both pieces of wood straight.

HELPFUL TIPS

- Make sure the dowel is ⅛ to ¼ inch shorter than the combined length of the drilled holes. This compensates for any hole depth errors and eliminates having to drill again.
- Mark the drill bit depth with tape so you know when to stop.
- Coat the dowel with woodworking glue before inserting. The glue adds strength to the joint.

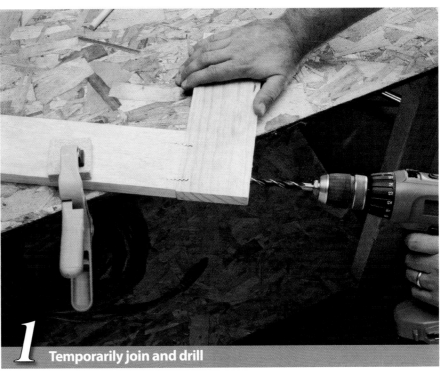

1 Temporarily join and drill

Position the boards the way you want them and join them temporarily with fasteners or clamps. If you use fasteners, make sure they are not in the way of the dowels. Square up the corner and drill holes for the dowels.

2 Drive the dowels and trim off

Squirt carpenter's glue into the drill holes and insert the dowels. Tap them all the way in and clean away excess glue. Cut off the dowels as flush with the board as possible without scratching the edge. Sand the remainder smooth.

Fastening with a biscuit joiner

- **TIME:** About 30 minutes to make two joints with eight biscuits
- **SKILLS:** Using power tools, particularly aligning a biscuit joiner and holding it flat
- **TOOLS:** Biscuit joiner, hammer, clamps, square

Biscuits—oval-shaped pieces of pressed wood—fit into slots cut by a biscuit joiner. With a biscuit joiner (sometimes called a "plate joiner") you can join boards edge to edge or edge to face, join ¾ inch or thicker edging to plywood, or make butt and miter joints.

The key to a strong joint with flush surfaces is the precise location of the slots in the wood. A rigid fence on the biscuit joiner ensures that the slots are cut the same distance from the joining surfaces. Coating the biscuit with glue causes it to swell slightly, creating a tight, strong joint.

Lay out the parts and mark the biscuit locations. Hold the tool with its base perfectly flat against the board as you make the cuts. If you are using more than three or four biscuits on a joint, work fast and have a helper on hand. Wear hearing protection and safety glasses. Keep hands and loose clothing away from the tool.

Edge-to-edge joints

Use biscuits when edge-gluing. Biscuits both strengthen a joint and help align the board surfaces. Place glue along the entire edge of the joint to create a strong bond. The boards should be at least ½ inch thick so the biscuits don't create surface bulges. On boards greater than 1 inch thick, you can cut two pockets for extra strength. Lay out the biscuit slots so they won't be exposed.

Corner butt joints

Clamp a support board onto the workpiece. Adjust the front fence so it is perpendicular to the surface being prepared. Lay the joiner onto the workpiece. Align the indicator mark with your layout line. Use both hands on the tool to keep it steady when you cut the slot.

T-joints

A biscuit joint can take the place of a dado when building fixed shelves. Mark layout lines on the workpiece to show where the matching board joins. Clamp a temporary wood fence onto the board. The joiner cuts the slots at the proper offset so the pieces match up.

CAUTION

USE BISCUIT JOINER SAFELY
The biscuit joiner blade safely retracts when not in use. When in use, the blade buries itself into the wood. Still, use caution when operating the tool. Wear hearing protection and safety glasses. Keep hands and loose clothing away from the tool when in operation.

1 Mark and cut

Position the boards as you want them joined. For every place you want to install a biscuit, mark a line running across the joint. Set the tool to the correct depth for the size of biscuit you're using. Hold the tool flat against the board as you make each slot.

2 Glue, join, and clamp

After dry-fitting the boards with the biscuits in place, apply carpenter's glue to the joint and put some glue into each slot. Set the biscuits into the slots on one board and slide them into their respective slots on the second board, tapping the board into place. Check that the joint is tight, then clamp. Wipe away excess glue and allow to dry.

Applying laminate

- **TIME:** About half a day to cover a couple of straightforward countertops
- **SKILLS:** Accurately measuring and cutting, applying cement smoothly, using a router
- **TOOLS:** Circular saw or carbide-tipped knife; brush, paint roller, or notched trowel; rolling pin; router, file, or sanding block

Plastic laminate comes in a variety of colors, patterns, and textures. With practice and the right tools, you can lay down laminate as well, if not as quickly, as a professional installer.

Be sure that the surface you are attaching the laminate to is straight, smooth, and supported so it will not flex. New particleboard works best, although laminate also can be applied to plywood and old laminate.

You can install laminate tops

Working with laminate is well within the realm of the do-it-yourselfer, unlike more expensive countertop options such as solid-surface materials or granite, where installation is best left to the pros. Laminate is available in myriad finishes and colors, making it an attractive option for countertops.

TOOLS TO USE

- A router with a special laminate-edging bit gives you smooth, professional-looking edges that you can't get with a sanding block or file. Experiment with the router on scrap pieces to set the bit to the correct depth. If it is too deep, you cut away too much and ruin the project.
- For small jobs or for areas the router can't reach, use a sanding block or a file. Work slowly. If you sand away too much laminate, the only way to fix it is to start over.

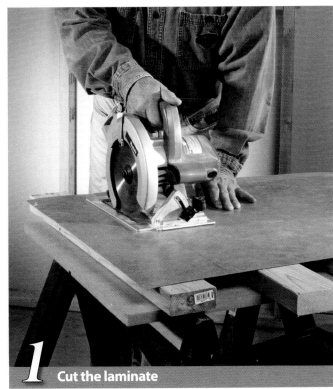

1 Cut the laminate

Cut the laminate so it is about ½ inch longer and wider than the surface to be covered; you'll trim it exactly after installing it. Cut the laminate with a circular saw or score its face with a carbide-tipped knife. Cut with the face up if you are using a tablesaw or with the face down if you are using a circular saw.

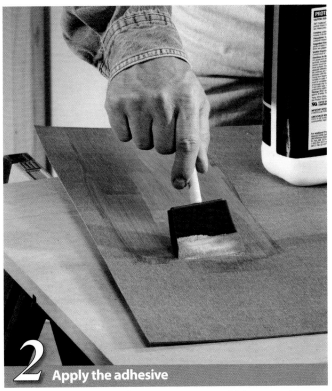

2 Apply the adhesive

Choose professional-grade contact cement, which costs a bit more than the homeowner-type cement. Spread it evenly onto the back of the laminate and the base surface using a brush, a paint roller, or a notched trowel. Allow both surfaces to dry completely before adhering the laminate.

Applying laminate *(continued)*

ADHESIVE CHOICES

Contact cement is not the only adhesive for laminates. Many fabricators, especially those working with large surfaces, use polyvinyl acetate glue (PVA). This milky-white glue forms a stronger bond than contact cement but lacks the water resistance. Yellow carpenter's glue, an aliphatic resin, is an offshoot of PVA. It works well on small projects such as shelving or backsplashes. Standard carpenter's glue is not waterproof, but some formulations of yellow glue are.

CAUTION

TAKE SAFETY PRECAUTIONS WHEN USING ADHESIVES

Many adhesive products for applying laminate contain volatile organic compounds (VOC). When inhaled, the compounds enter your bloodstream. Temporary exposure to VOC can cause dizziness, headaches, and nausea. Continued and frequent exposure could lead to debilitating health problems, including permanent damage to the nervous system, kidneys, and liver.

Information about toxic elements and how to protect against them is available. Ask the supplier for a Material Safety Data Sheet (MSDS) for the product. This form provides the detailed information on toxicity, correct handling, proper protective gear, and proper disposal of the product. Federal regulations require all suppliers to have these forms available and to provide you with a copy upon request.

Always work in a well-ventilated area when using these products. Use an appropriate mask. Dust masks are useless when it comes to stopping inhalation of VOCs. Respirators with VOC-approved cartridges are the only effective filters for toxic fumes. Ask your local auto supply store, lumberyard, or home center for the appropriate mask.

3 Attach the laminate

Cover the surface with brown wrapping paper and lay the laminate on top. (You also can separate the base and laminate with dowels or sticks.) When the laminate is positioned, carefully pull out the paper or supports. Roll the surface from the middle outward with a rolling pin.

4 Attach edging, and trim

Attach the edging pieces so they butt tightly against the underside of the laminate piece. To finish the project, trim the overhanging edges of laminate with a router, file, or sanding block. Take care not to crack the laminate or lift it up as you work.

Shaping and planing

Beveling edges and corners, fitting doors, and trueing edges and ends of lumber—most carpentry projects include at least one of these shaping tasks. The three best types of tools for shaping wood surfaces are planes, surface-forming tools, and rasps or wood files. With practice and a clean, sharp tool, shaping can be a pleasure rather than a chore.

However, even the sharpest tools are no match for a board that's badly twisted, bowed, cupped, or warped (see page 84). Always inspect your material for flaws and select only stock suitable for the job. Don't assume you can shape it up later.

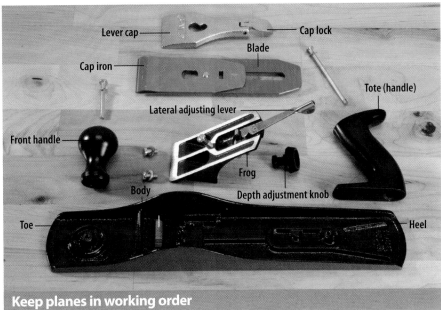

Lever cap — Cap lock — Blade — Cap iron — Tote (handle) — Lateral adjusting lever — Front handle — Frog — Body — Depth adjustment knob — Toe — Heel

Keep planes in working order

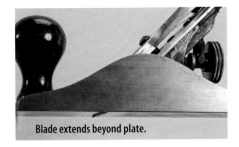

Blade extends beyond plate.

Various types and sizes of planes are available. Most carpenters use a smoothing plane or jack plane (shown above) and a block plane (see page 54). To help keep the blade sharp, lay the plane on its side when not in use.

Retract the blade into the body for storage. If any parts become rusty, clean them with a little oil and fine steel wool. Adjust the blade so it cuts thin shavings easily; you should not have to fight against the wood.

Follow general planing rules

- It takes both hands to push the plane smoothly, so clamp your work.
- Plane with the grain.
- When planing a narrow edge, grip a square-cornered block of wood against the bottom of the plane as you work, as shown above.

- If you get anything but a continuous, even shaving, the blade is dull, adjusted too thick, or going against the grain.
- To avoid nicking corners, apply pressure to the knob at the front of the tool at the beginning of your cut and to the handle at the end of the cut.

SCRIBING A TRUE LINE

To straighten a piece of lumber or a door, you must first draw the line indicating where the piece should end. This is called a true line. A true line is usually straight, but not always. For instance, a door often must be planed to fit an opening that is not straight. To make a true line, scribe it by holding the piece up against the place into which it must fit. Run your pencil along the opening as you mark the piece for planing.

When scribing a line, check the angle at which you are holding the pencil and the thickness of the pencil line. Hold the pencil at the same angle at all points along your scribe line or you will cut off too little or too much wood. Decide if you want to cut off all of the pencil mark or just up to the mark.

Shaping and planing *(continued)*

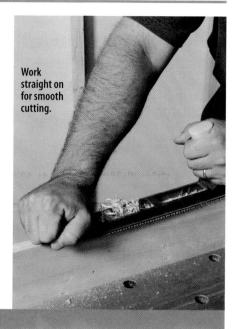

Work straight on for smooth cutting.

Shape with surface-forming tools

Surface-forming tools come in a variety of sizes and shapes. The one shown above works much like a plane. You cannot adjust the depth of the cut, and it will not produce as smooth a cut as a plane, but it is easy to use.

You can regulate the cut by the way you position the tool against the material. For rough-cutting, hold the tool at a 45-degree angle to the work as you push the tool. For a smoother result, hold the tool parallel to the board's edge.

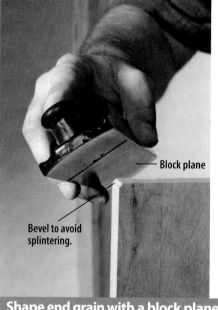

Block plane

Bevel to avoid splintering.

End grain

Shape end grain with a block plane

As long as you're shaping wood parallel to the grain, planing will go smoothly. But when you need to shape the end grain, you will be working at a 90-degree angle to the grain. A block plane with a low blade angle works best on end

grain. Bevel the corners first, with the bottom of the bevel at the final cutline. Plane from both edges to the center to prevent splintering the edges. On narrow stock, clamp scrap wood against one edge to support the grain, and plane in that direction.

Sanding

Once you've taken the time to cut and assemble your project, don't skimp when it comes to the final steps. Do a thorough job of sanding so the wood will be well-prepared for its finish. Don't expect stain, varnish, or paint to smooth out the surface for you; they follow the contours of the wood and often accentuate, rather than hide, imperfections. Unless you are using a belt sander with a rough abrasive, don't try to remove more than $1/32$ inch of material by sanding; shape or plane instead (see pages 53–54).

Use a belt sander for rough work

Use this tool only on rough surfaces and only if you are sure of yourself; it is easy to make gouges if you tip the tool or if you rest it in one spot too long. Always run the sander with the grain, never across it. Don't apply pressure as you work; just let the weight of the sander do the work.

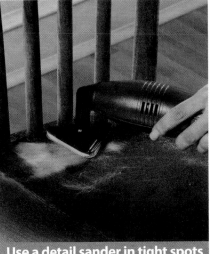

Use a detail sander in tight spots

For awkward areas, a detail sander can spare you hours of fingertip work. Sanding pads are self-adhesive or have hook-and-loop backing; just lift one off and put on the next one. Work carefully. A detail sander has oscillating action. Because it concentrates on such a small area, it takes off material quickly.

CAUTION

SAND SAFELY
Particularly when sanding with power tools, wear a dust mask. To avoid difficult cleanup later, seal the room.

Hand-sand with a block

Except in hard-to-reach areas, never use abrasive sheets alone—always use some sort of sanding block, either purchased or improvised. Sanding with a block is less tiring and produces more uniform results. Tear abrasive sheets to size rather than cut them or you will dull your knife blade quickly. Check that the bottom of your block is clean and smooth. Any debris can tear the paper and mar your work. Sand only in the direction of the wood grain. Sanding across the grain or in a circular motion can leave hard-to-remove scratches. Don't exert much pressure. If you're using the right grade of paper, light strokes are all you need.

SAND THREE TIMES

- Take the time and go to the trouble to sand three times, using progressively finer-grit sandpaper. The wood surface may feel smooth after your first and second sandings, but it will get smoother as you move on to finer-grit sandpapers. A common progression is to start with 80-grit paper, then proceed to 120-, 180-, and possibly even 240-grit abrasives. Clean dust from the wood between sandings.
- If you can't sand out a stain or discoloration, apply a small amount of laundry bleach to it. Try several applications until you get the right color. Let dry before sanding again.

Sanding (continued)

Wrap sandpaper around wood scrap.

Wind scrap of abrasive around finger.

Roll sandpaper around dowel.

Use ingenuity for tight spots

When smoothing wood in tight quarters or in unusual situations, special tools can help. Consider buying or renting a detail sander (see page 55) or a contour sanding attachment for your drill. Often, however, you can do the job with a sheet of abrasive and a little ingenuity, as the three examples above show.

To sand two surfaces where they meet at an inside corner, wrap a creased sheet of abrasive around a sharp-cornered block. To smooth inside edges of bored holes and small cutouts, wrap abrasive around your finger or a small round object. For sanding outside curves, wrap a sheet of abrasive around a dowel.

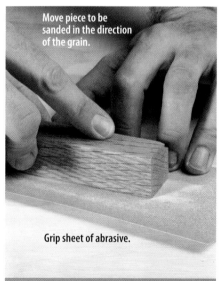

Move piece to be sanded in the direction of the grain.

Grip sheet of abrasive.

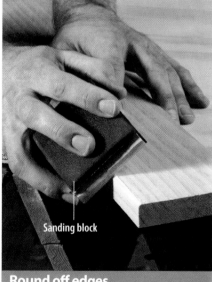

Sanding block

Masking tape

Sand a small piece

When you need to smooth a small item, sand it by sliding it over a full sheet of abrasive held flat with your free hand. This keeps the surface of the piece even and flat. If the abrasive fills with dust, wipe it with a clean cloth or give it a few slaps against your bench.

Round off edges

Sharp wood edges are susceptible to nicking and splintering, so it is a good idea to blunt them with a light sanding. Hold the sanding block at an angle; use gentle pressure combined with a rocking motion. A rubber sanding block like the one shown above is ideal for this purpose because it is slightly resilient.

Protect edges with tape

Sometimes you'll want to sand one surface without scratching an adjoining surface. To do this, apply masking tape to protect the surface you don't want sanded. Affix the tape carefully, making sure it adheres tightly at all points. Watch closely as you sand and immediately replace any tape that rips or gets damaged.

Filling and finishing

Paint, stain, and clear finishes rarely cover up imperfections in wood. Often they make things look worse rather than better. It pays to prepare your wood carefully before you add a finish.

Fill holes with wood filler, and sand the surface smooth. If you're applying a clear finish, limit your use of putty to small spots; even putty that is made to accept stain never quite looks like real wood. Even if you're going to paint the surface, cover exposed plywood edges. They soak up paint like a sponge and look rough no matter how many coats of paint you apply.

Once the wood surface is prepared, match your paint, stain, or clear finish to the intended use of your project. See the chart on page 58 for selecting finishes.

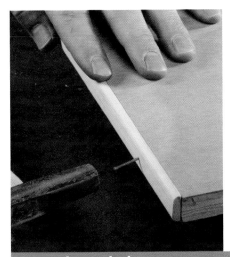
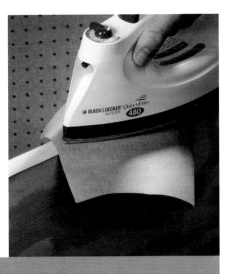

Cover plywood edges

To conceal a plywood edge, cut a thin piece of molding to fit, apply carpenter's glue to the edge, and fasten the molding with brads (small finishing nails). You also can cover an edge with wood veneer tape. Buy tape that is wider than the thickness of the material and that matches its surface. Cut the tape with scissors, leaving at least ¼ inch extra on all edges. Position iron-on tape carefully so it covers the edge along the entire length. Apply even, steady pressure with a household iron set on high.

Use contact cement to apply non-iron-on veneer. Trim the edges with a sharp knife, then lightly sand the corners.

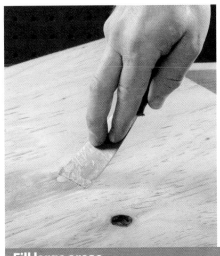
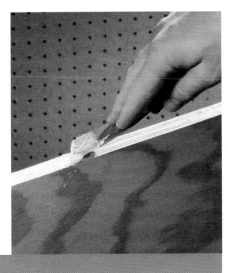

Fill nail and screw holes

For small holes, use a dough-type wood filler. Apply filler before or after staining; experiment to find out which looks best. Begin by tamping a small amount of the filler into the hole with your thumb. Smooth it with a putty knife. Wipe away the excess with a rag dampened with water or mineral spirits, depending on the type of putty. (Check manufacturer's directions.)

Fill large areas

If you're going to paint the entire surface of a project, water-mix putty excels at filling shallow depressions over a large surface area. The putty sets up quickly, so don't mix more than you can use in 10 minutes. To fill cracks around a knot, mix the putty to a pastelike consistency and force it into all the cracks with a putty knife. Feather out the patch to the surrounding wood. To fill edges of plywood or the end grain of boards, mix the putty to a thinner consistency. Sand and apply a second coat if necessary. For deep holes you may have to apply two layers to allow for any shrinkage of the first layer of putty.

Filling and finishing *(continued)*

SELECTING CLEAR FINISHES

Adhesive type	Characteristics	Application and drying time
Natural-resin varnish	Resists scratches, scuffs. Spar varnish good outdoors.	Use varnish brush or cheesecloth pad. Dries in 24–36 hours. In humid weather, allow 36 hours.
Polyurethane varnish	Resists marring, durable, remains clear.	Use natural-bristle brush, roller, or spray. Let dry 1–2 hours; 12 hours between coats.
Two-part epoxy varnish	High resistance to scuffs and mars. Ideal for floors.	Use brush. Check directions if coating wood filler. First coat dries in 3 hours, second in 5–8 hours.
Shellac	Easily damaged by water. Clear or pigmented.	Use small brush with chiseled tip. Thin with alcohol or recommended solvent. Dries in about 2 hours.
Lacquer	Fast-drying. Ideal for furniture.	Best sprayed on in many thin coats. Let last coat dry 48–60 hours, then rub with fine steel wool or hard wax.
Resin oil	Soaks into and hardens grain. Resists scratches.	Usually hand-rubbed in 2–3 coats. Needs 8–12 hours to dry.

Apply penetrating stain

Apply stain with a brush and wait for a few minutes. The heavier the application and the longer you wait, the deeper the color. Wipe with a clean rag, taking care to make the color even throughout the piece. To make it darker, apply a second coat. If it is too dark, rub with a cloth moistened with the recommended thinner.

Begin with strokes across the grain.

Finish with long strokes with the grain.

Paint correctly for a smooth look

Painting with a brush may seem like a simple task, but here are a few tips to keep in mind. Begin applying paint to wood surfaces with short strokes across the wood grain, laying down paint in both directions. Don't bear down too hard on the bristles.

Finish painting with longer, sweeping strokes in one direction only—this time with the wood grain. Use just the tips of the bristles to smooth out the paint.

ANTIQUING

If you have worn or marred furniture or cabinets, you can avoid all the work of stripping, sanding, and refinishing them by emphasizing imperfections in the wood.

If you are new to this process, buy an antiquing kit, which usually includes base- and finish-coating materials and brushes and applicators. Choose from a variety of finishes: marbleized, distressed, spattered, stippled, crumpled, and others.

Remove dirt and wax from the surface, apply the base coat, and let it dry. After sanding, quickly apply a finish coat. Wipe it to achieve the desired finish. Let dry 48 hours and add a clear, protective finish.

CARPENTRY

Building a wall

■ **TIME:** About 2 hours to build a simple 10-foot wall, longer if you need to build it in place or in an awkward location

■ **SKILLS:** Measuring, cutting, fastening with nails

■ **TOOLS:** Tape measure, chalkline, pencil, framing square, saw, speed or combination square, level, hammer

Most residential walls are built with vertical members (studs) that butt against horizontal members (plates) at the top and bottom. Although it looks straightforward, building a wall takes some planning. When you cover the framing with sheets of drywall or paneling, the seams between sheets must fall at the center of studs. In addition, nailing surfaces must be provided for the sheets at all the corners (see page 63), and all framing members must be aligned along a flat plane.

If the floor and ceiling are nearly level, it's easy to preassemble a stud wall on the floor and tilt it into position. If the floor and ceiling are uneven or if you're building the wall in tight quarters, it's best to build the wall in place, custom-cutting each stud to fit, and toenailing it to the top and bottom plates (see pages 62–63).

Whichever approach you choose, consider how you attach your wall to the ceiling. If the wall runs perpendicularly to the ceiling joists, simply fasten the wall's top plate with two 16d nails at every joist. If it runs parallel to the joists, you have to place the wall under a joist or install blocking between joists so you can nail the top plate into solid material.

GETTING THE STUD LENGTH CORRECT

Few things are more frustrating than building a stud wall only to find that your measurements were off and the wall is ¼ inch too tall. When that happens, the only thing you can do is lay the wall down, pull off one plate, remove the nails, cut all the studs, and nail the wall back together again.

To measure for stud length, nail together two scraps of 2×4 to represent the top and bottom plates. Set this double 2×4 on the floor, measure up to the joist, and subtract ¼ inch for shimming. Take measurements every few feet.

1 Mark the wall location

Begin by deciding exactly where the wall will go. Use a framing square and a chalkline to mark its location on the floor. Check long walls for square using the 3-4-5 method (see page 14).

Using a level and a straight 2×4 that is as long as your ceiling height, mark the wall location on the ceiling, joists, or crossbracing. These marks help you position the wall before you plumb it. Make sure there is adequate framing in the ceiling to which you can nail the top plate.

2 Cut and mark the plates

Using your floor layout as a guide, mark and cut 2×4s for the top and bottom plates (usually the same length). Place them on edge beside each other and mark for the studs. The first stud should be at the end of the wall. Position the center of the next stud 16 inches from the end of the wall. Place remaining studs 16 inches on center (OC) so the distance from the center of one stud to the next is 16 inches. With a combination or speed square, draw lines ¾ inch on each side of your stud centers. Draw an X between the marks to show where to nail the studs.

3 Provide nailers; cut studs

If your new wall runs parallel to the ceiling joists cut pieces of 2× material to fit tightly between the ceiling joists and install them every 2 feet or so. Measure for your studs and cut them to length.

4 Assemble the wall

Working on a flat surface, lay the studs on edge between the top and bottom plates. It helps to have something solid, such as a wall, to hold the framing against while you assemble and nail the wall.

5 Raise the frame

Framework can be cumbersome, so have a helper on hand. Position the bottom plate about where it needs to go and tip the wall into position. If the wall fits so tightly against the ceiling that you have to hammer it into place, protect the framing with a scrap of 2×4 as you pound. Tap both ends of the frame until it is roughly plumb in both directions.

6 Snug the frame with shims

If the wall is a bit short in places, drive shims between the bottom plate and the floor or between the top plate and the ceiling joists. Shimming the top is best. Have your helper steady the framework while you drive the pieces into place. Drive shims from both sides, thin edge to thin edge, to keep the plate from tilting.

7 Fasten frame to wall and floor

After the frame is snug, recheck that the wall is plumb in both directions. Check both ends of the wall and every other stud. Fasten the top plate to the ceiling by driving a 16d nail through the plate and into each joist or nailer. Fasten the bottom plate to the floor. Use 16d nails if the floor is wood; use masonry nails or a power hammer if the floor is concrete.

Building a wall in place

- **TIME:** About 4 to 5 hours, depending on the size of the wall
- **SKILLS:** Measuring, leveling, and plumbing; drilling and driving screws; shimming
- **TOOLS:** Tape measure, level, framing square, chalkline, plumb line, hammer

If building a wall on the floor and raising it into position is not practical in your situation, construct the wall in place. The main complication to building in place is toenailing the studs top and bottom. You must measure and cut the studs carefully too so they fit between the solidly nailed plates.

Typically walls are built with 2×4 framing lumber. Existing or new plumbing may require more space than provided in a standard wall. Use 2×6 framing lumber to build a wall that will contain large plumbing such as waste pipes. When wall plates are spaced around pipes or mechanical fixtures, join the framing members with metal straps.

Building walls with metal studs (pages 64–65) offers an alternative to standard wooden construction and can be easier to build in place.

Before covering any new wall with drywall, have the local building inspector check the construction. The inspector makes sure that plumbing and wiring are properly installed, so have them in place and exposed for review. Few things are more time-consuming, expensive, and frustrating than having to remove drywall so the building inspector can check the work.

QUIETER WALLS

To insulate against sound, build a wall with 2×6 top and bottom plates and staggered 2×4 studs. Purchase fiberglass insulation in batts or rolls and weave it between the studs along the length of the wall. Fill to the full height of the studs. The insulation establishes a barrier that reduces din and provides a quiet sanctuary. Add insulation board under the drywall for an additional noise barrier.

Soundproof drywall, though expensive, provides the greatest sound control for home theaters and studios.

1 Install top and bottom plates

Cut the top and bottom plates and mark them for stud locations (see page 60). Transfer the marks to the faces of the plates, making sure the marks are clear so you can see them easily to align the studs while toenailing.

If the ceiling is unfinished, finding the joists is easy. If the ceiling is finished, you need to locate them. Use a stud finder to locate the first joist. Mark both sides of the joist. The rest of the joists should be on 16-inch centers, so you can measure to locate them. Double-check the location with the stud finder.

Nail the top plate to the joists. Use a level and a straight board or a plumb line to mark the location of the bottom plate, or use a chalkline case as a plumb bob. Mark the floor in two places and make an X to indicate on which side of the mark the plate should be positioned. Use masonry nails or a power hammer to fasten the bottom plate to the floor.

2 Cut and position the studs

With top and bottom plates installed, measure the required length of each stud individually. Add $\frac{1}{16}$ inch for a snug fit and cut. Tap each stud into place. If you really have to whack it to get it into place, it is too long. Don't risk splitting the stud; take it down and trim it a little. To secure the studs, drive 8d nails at an angle through the side of studs and into the plate; this is called toenailing. Tap the nail once or twice while holding it parallel to the floor or ceiling. When the nail tip bites into the wood, change the angle to 45 degrees.

Temporary brace

3 Toenail the studs

Drive four to six nails into each joint, two on each side, with an optional one at the front and back. The first nail may move the stud, but the second nail, driven from the other side, will move it back.

If you have difficulty toenailing, drill pilot holes for the nails using a $\frac{3}{32}$-inch bit. Or place a $14\frac{1}{2}$-inch board between studs to serve as a temporary nailing brace. Push the stud against the brace and nail one side. Then remove the brace and nail the other side.

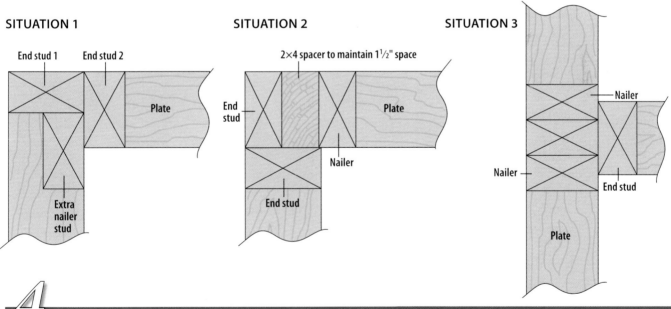

SITUATION 1

End stud 1 · End stud 2 · Plate · Extra nailer stud

SITUATION 2

2×4 spacer to maintain $1\frac{1}{2}$" space · End stud · Plate · Nailer · End stud

SITUATION 3

Nailer · Nailer · End stud · Plate

4 Frame at corners

When framing corners, make sure there is a nailing surface for every piece of drywall or paneling that will be installed. This means adding nonstructural nailers.

In Situation 1, above, left, the extra stud is turned sideways to offer a nailing surface and strengthen the corner. Drive 16d nails first through end stud 1 and into the extra stud, then through end stud 2 and into the extra stud and end stud 1.

In Situation 2, above, middle, several foot-long 2×4 scraps (usually three in a standard 8-foot wall) serve as spacers between two full-length studs placed at the end of one wall. Tie the wall sections together with 16d nails.

Situation 3, above, right, shows two intersecting walls. Nail three studs together and to the plates, then attach to the adjoining wall.

63

Working with metal studs

- **TIME:** 1 to 2 hours to build a basic 12-foot wall
- **SKILLS:** Measuring and marking for walls, cutting with tin snips, fastening with a drill or screw gun
- **TOOLS:** Tape measure, level, tin snips or circular saw with metal-cutting blade, chalkline, drill or screw gun, plumb bob

Metal framing costs a good deal less than wood 2×4s, and it is lighter. Metal is not susceptible to rot or insect damage, and the factory-made pieces are free from bows, twists, knots, and other imperfections that sometimes make wood hard to work with.

Working with metal studs takes some adjustments. You can't build walls on the floor and then raise them up. Instead you must install the top and floor runners, then insert the studs.

Cut metal studs with tin snips or a circular saw fitted with a metal-cutting blade. Fasten the pieces together with self-tapping screws.

If you make a mistake, it usually is easier to move a metal stud than a wood one. Electrical wiring and pipes for plumbing are easy to run through precut punch-out holes in the studs.

Once walls are built, however, you can't attach items to metal stud walls as easily as you can to wood walls. You can fasten items to a metal stud with a screw but not a nail. If you plan to hang cabinets or shelves on the wall, crossbrace the wall with C-runners or 2×4 blocking. Door jambs and windows can be attached to steel framing. But it's easier to shim and attach the units if you use wood framing, fastened to the metal studs, around these openings.

1 Cut the runners

Lay out the framing as you would for a wood wall (see pages 62–63). With tin snips cut the runners to be used for top and bottom plates to length. Or use a metal-cutting blade on a circular saw. A circular saw is faster but throws metal filings. Make sure no one is in the area as you cut and wear protective eyewear and clothing as you work.

2 Attach the ceiling runner

Position the ceiling runner and attach it to each joist with a 2-inch drywall screw. If joists run parallel to the wall, install crossmembers, to which you can attach the runner. Using a plumb bob, position the floor runner directly below the ceiling runner. Attach it to the floor with screws or masonry nails.

CAUTION

METAL STUDS ARE SHARP

The ends of metal studs, especially those that you cut, often are very sharp. When working with metal, wear gloves. If you're cutting with a circular saw and metal-cutting blade, wear long sleeves that are not loose or floppy.

Cutting metal also can be dangerous because small pieces of metal fly through the air. Be sure to wear eye protection whenever you cut metal studs.

If you run electrical wiring through metal framing, use sections of plastic foam pipe insulation or specially made plastic grommets to protect wires from damage.

3 Cut and insert the studs

Cut the studs to length with tin snips. Insert them into the runners, starting at a slight angle and twisting them into place. For easier plumbing or electrical installation, make sure all the stud legs point in the same direction and all the predrilled punchouts line up.

4 Attach studs to the runners

Once studs are placed correctly, drive $7/16$-inch pan- or wafer-head screws through the runners into the studs. Hold the stud flange firmly against the runner as you work. Drive four screws, one on either side of each stud at the top and bottom.

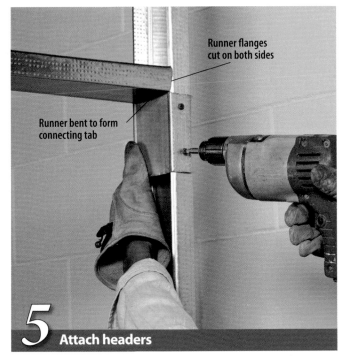

Runner flanges cut on both sides

Runner bent to form connecting tab

5 Attach headers

Where you need a door or window header, cut a piece of runner 8 inches longer than the width of the opening. Cut the two sides of the runner 4 inches from each end so you can bend back a tab, as shown. Slip the tabs into place and attach with screws.

6 Install the drywall

Inspect the framing to make sure you have a fastening surface for drywall at all points. Attach the drywall with drywall screws placed 8 to 12 inches apart. Install corner beads with screws or staples. Tape and finish the walls (see pages 72–73).

Furring basement walls

- **TIME:** 1 day for a 12×12-foot room
- **SKILLS:** Laying out, measuring, cutting, hammering
- **TOOLS:** Hammer, baby sledge, caulking gun, circular saw, tape measure, level, chalkline

When finishing basement walls, you can build stud walls (see pages 60–63) and fasten them to the concrete or masonry walls. A stud wall goes up quickly, gives you room to add plenty of insulation, and ensures that the new walls will be straight, even if the existing walls are not. However, you lose some floor space because of the thickness of the walls.

If insulation is not a problem and your basement walls are smooth and straight, you can save money in materials and preserve some square footage by fastening 1×2, 1×3, or 1×4 furring strips to the walls.

The layout is the same as it is for stud walls. The ends of drywall or paneling sheets and all joints must fall on a furring strip, and there must be nailing surfaces at all corners.

The construction method, however, is different. Furring strips are individually attached to the wall (shimmed where necessary) with glue and masonry nails or with a power hammer, which shoots nails with gunpowder charges (see page 67).

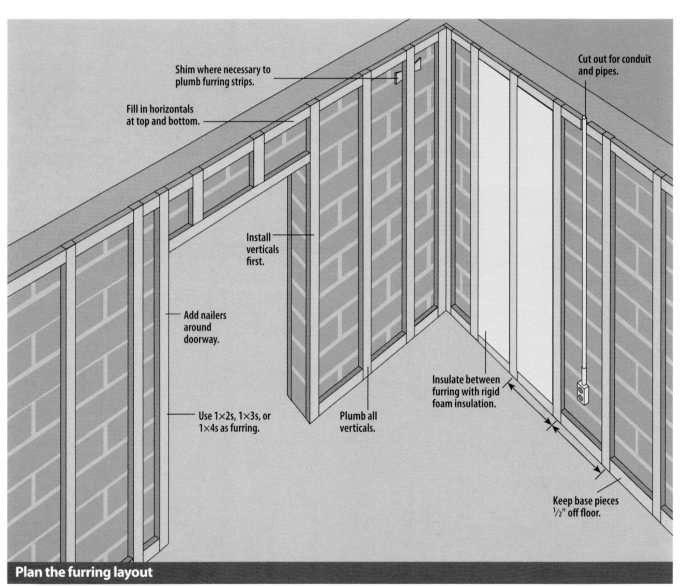

Shim where necessary to plumb furring strips.

Fill in horizontals at top and bottom.

Install verticals first.

Add nailers around doorway.

Use 1×2s, 1×3s, or 1×4s as furring.

Plumb all verticals.

Cut out for conduit and pipes.

Insulate between furring with rigid foam insulation.

Keep base pieces ½" off floor.

Plan the furring layout

Begin the job by marking the locations of the vertical furring strips. One easy way to do this is to position a sheet of your wall material in the corner of the room, plumb it, and strike a chalkline down its outside edge to mark the centerline for one strip. Using this line as a guide and 16 inches as the center-to-center measurement, mark the locations of the other vertical strips along that wall.

Measure and cut each strip to fit between the floor and ceiling. Cut each piece ½ inch short so that it will be fastened a bit above the floor as a safeguard against moisture.

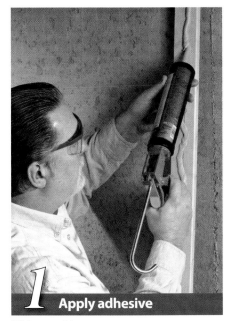

1 Apply adhesive

With a caulking gun, squeeze a wavy ¼-inch bead of construction adhesive onto the furring strip. As you finish, release the pressure on the adhesive, discontinuing the flow. Push the strip against the wall in its correct location, pressing firmly to help spread the adhesive.

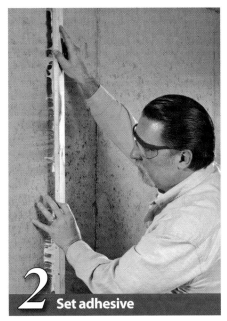

2 Set adhesive

Pull the strip off the wall and lean it against another wall to let the adhesive begin to set up. After letting it set for the time specified by the manufacturer, press the strip back into place.

3 Plumb and shim

Check the strip for plumb. If a dip or bulge is noticeable, tuck pairs of shims behind the strip and wedge it into line. Double-check your work as the job progresses by holding a straightedge horizontally across four or five vertical pieces. Correct any gaps or bulges.

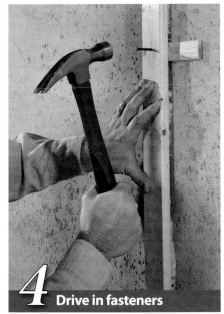

4 Drive in fasteners

Hammer concrete nails through the strip and the shims and into the masonry wall. On a brick or block wall, it often is easiest to drive the nails into the mortar joints. Use a baby sledge if you have one. Hand-driving nails into concrete walls is extremely difficult; consider a power hammer (see "Tools to Use," right).

5 Add the horizontals

After all the verticals are in place, aligned, and secured, begin work on the top and bottom horizontal pieces. Measure and cut them one at a time. Apply adhesive, shim if necessary, and install them as you installed the verticals.

TOOLS TO USE

A power hammer makes basement remodeling easier. It's usually better to rent a better-quality power tool than to buy a cheap one. Experiment with several types of loads to find one powerful enough to drive the nails in but not so powerful as to drive them completely through the furring strips. Note: Follow the manufacturer's directions carefully. A power hammer is closely related to a firearm and is dangerous if misused.

On large jobs, a large-tube caulking gun pays for itself because adhesive purchased in large tubes costs less per ounce. It also saves you time and creates less mess because big tubes contain more than twice as much as the smaller tubes.

Laying out and cutting drywall

- **TIME:** With a helper, 1 day for a 12×12-foot room
- **SKILLS:** Measuring, physical strength, thoroughness
- **TOOLS:** Tape measure, drywall square, utility knife, drywall saw, chalkline

Drywall is inexpensive, and any homeowner has the skills needed to hang and finish it. But hanging drywall is tiring work. The sheets are heavy and unwieldy. Making cutouts for electrical boxes and pipes can be tedious. Careful installation makes finishing easier.

Finishing drywall to a smooth surface requires three applications of compound and sanding for professional installers—perhaps more for amateurs. Some homeowners prefer to have a professional install and finish drywall.

Check framing to make sure you have adequate nailing surfaces (see page 70). Add framing members where you need them. If you are covering an existing wall, locate the joists and studs and clearly mark their locations on the walls and ceiling. A helper is essential—hanging drywall alone is nearly impossible.

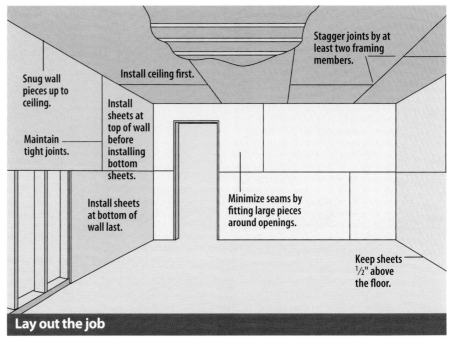

Stagger joints by at least two framing members.

Install ceiling first.

Snug wall pieces up to ceiling.

Install sheets at top of wall before installing bottom sheets.

Maintain tight joints.

Install sheets at bottom of wall last.

Minimize seams by fitting large pieces around openings.

Keep sheets ½" above the floor.

Lay out the job

To hold the sheets off the floor, store drywall sheets flat or on edge on pieces of 1× or 2× scrap lumber. Before cutting a sheet, make sure the finished surface faces you.

DRYWALL SQUARE

Don't hesitate to spend the money for a drywall square (see page 76). It quickly pays for itself in time and labor savings. For crosscuts, you simply make one measurement, set the square in place, and run your knife along the square's blade for a square cut. It also simplifies rip cuts (see page 69).

1 Make a crosscut

Mark your cutline, stand the sheet on edge, and set your drywall square in place. Clasp the square firmly on top and brace it at its base with your foot. With the edge of the knife blade against the square, cut downward most of the way, then finish by cutting up from the bottom.

2 Snap to cut

Snap the segment back away from your cutline. Finally slice through the backing paper with your knife.

3 Measure for the last piece

To determine the correct cutoff length of a corner sheet, measure the distance from the last sheet to the corner at both the top and the bottom. If the corner is more than ¼ inch out of square, mark both ends of the cut rather than make a square cut using a drywall square.

4 Make a rip cut …

If you need to make a parallel rip cut—one that is the same width all along its length—use your drywall square. Set the square on the edge of the sheet and hold the knife against it at the measured distance. Slide the square along with the knife, cutting as you go.

or a freehand cut

Often a rip cut is not square; it is shorter at one end. In this case, make a mark at each end of the sheet and chalk a line between the marks. Cut freehand or use a straightedge as a guide if you need a more precise edge.

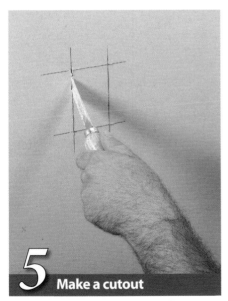

5 Make a cutout

To make a cutout for an electrical box, measure from the box edges to the edge of the last panel. Measure from the top and bottom of the box to the bottom of the sheet of drywall above it or the ceiling. Transfer the measurements to the sheet and draw a rectangle. Score the surface with a utility knife, then cut it with a drywall saw.

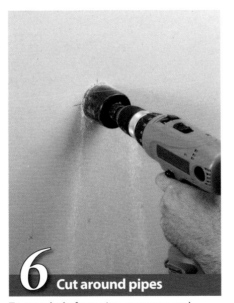

6 Cut around pipes

To cut a hole for a pipe, measure and mark the sheet for the center of the pipe. Drill a hole using a holesaw bit that is slightly larger than the pipe diameter. Or draw a circle and cut it out with a drywall saw or a knife.

AVOID MOISTURE DAMAGE IN A BASEMENT

Wood framing can withstand occasional wetness as long as it is allowed to dry out, but drywall that gets wet once loses its strength and crumbles.

When you are drywalling a basement or another place that is subject to chronic dampness or occasional flooding, add nailers to the base of the framing and cut the drywall sheets so they are held off the floor 2 to 3 inches. When you install the baseboard molding, add furring to fill the gap.

If your basement is subject to more drastic flooding, raise the drywall even higher. To do this, install a 1×6 baseboard directly onto the framing and set the drywall on top of it. This keeps the drywall 5½ inches above the floor.

Hanging drywall

- **TIME:** 20 minutes per sheet for walls, 30 minutes per ceiling sheet
- **SKILLS:** A strong back, fastening in difficult circumstances
- **TOOLS:** Tape measure, good ladders or scaffolding, hammer or drill with drywall-type screwdriver attachment, drywall taping blades

Be prepared for strenuous labor when you hang drywall. The sheets are heavy, you often have to work in awkward positions, and you have to hold the sheets in place while you drive nails or screws. It's tempting to rush the job, but sloppy installation makes finishing more difficult. Wide gaps between drywall sheets take a long time to tape, and nobody wants nails popping out later. Here's how to do the job correctly the first time.

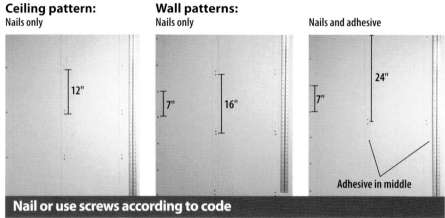

Ceiling pattern: Nails only

Wall patterns: Nails only

Nails and adhesive

12"

7" 16"

24"

7"

Adhesive in middle

Nail or use screws according to code

Local building codes specify how many nails or screws to use to hang drywall and in what sort of pattern. Codes vary not only from region to region, but also from room to room; for example, more fasteners may be required in bathrooms. Check with your building department. Many professionals don't nail in pairs, but there is good reason to do so: If one nail pops through the paper, the other holds. For ceiling panels, the general practice is to pair nails at 12-inch intervals around the perimeter and every 12 inches along each joist. When using adhesive, install two nails at 24-inch intervals and one nail every 7 inches along the edge. Keep adhesive 6 inches away from the edges of the sheets.

Requirements are less stringent for walls. If you don't use adhesive, install two nails into the wall studs at 16-inch intervals and a single nail every 7 inches along edges.

Attach drywall with screws

The screw head must be set below the surface, but it must not break the paper. This is difficult to do with a simple screwdriver bit. Use a dimpler bit or a drywall screwdriver (see "Tools to Use" on opposite page). Always drive in screws perpendicularly to the sheet, or their heads will tear the paper.

WRONG: Nailhead protrudes.

CORRECT: Nailhead set in dimple.

WRONG: Paper broken.

Set nailheads correctly

If you simply drive a nail flush, you will not be able to hide it with joint compound. If you drive the nail too deeply, you will break the paper on the drywall. When the paper is broken, the nail won't hold; it tears right through the gypsum inner core. Drive the nail so the nailhead is set into a slightly dimpled surface. No portion of the nailhead should protrude above the surface of the drywall. To test if your nails are driven deeply enough, run a taping blade along the surface of the wall. You should not feel any nailheads click against the blade as you pull it across. Pull out any nails that miss a joist or stud; swat the hole with your hammer to dimple it.

Install the ceiling sheets

TOOLS TO USE

Hammers made especially for drywall installation are light for easy handling. They have wide heads so it's easier to make a dimple without damaging the paper, and their heads are tilted a bit for access to corners. You may not use one very often, but it will make hanging and, subsequently, taping drywall easier.

A drywall screwdriver has an adjustable bit that, once set correctly, will drive a screw to the correct depth, then stop. A less expensive but just as good option is a dimpler bit that you can attach to any electric drill.

Hang drywall on the ceiling before installing the wall sheets. Start in a corner and work out from there, keeping the panels perpendicular to the joists. Before you start, take time to locate joists and mark their locations on the sheet and the wall. Searching for joists while holding the sheet up with your head is no fun.

The quickest but most difficult way to install drywall on a ceiling is to set the panel in place and support it with your head, leaving your hands free to hold and drive nails or screws. Wearing a baseball cap greatly minimizes pulled hair and a sore head.

To make hanging drywall easier, construct one or two 2×2 T-braces to use as props or rent a drywall hoist (see inset, above). Either solution makes the process easier and results in a much neater job.

Install the wall sheets

Ceiling corner

Nail 7" from ceiling corner.

Ceiling joist

Inside corner

Place first.

Place first.

Outside corner

Once the ceiling panels are up, hang sheets on the walls. If you are installing sheets horizontally, begin with the upper sheets, butting them firmly against the ceiling drywall. Make sure all vertical seams hit studs. Butt the lower panels firmly against the upper panels, tapered edge to tapered edge. Raise sheets tightly with a wedge or lever.

If you are installing sheets vertically, check that the tapered edges fall midway across a stud. If they don't, either cut the drywall or attach pieces of lumber to the stud to give yourself a nailing surface for the next piece.

Overlap pieces at corners, as shown above. Finish the job by adding the filler pieces, measuring and cutting each piece to size. Make sure each piece has at least two nailing members to support it.

Taping drywall

- **TIME:** For a typical bedroom, 5 hours for the first coat and 2 hours for subsequent coats, plus time for sanding and drying
- **SKILLS:** Patience and willingness to learn
- **TOOLS:** Utility knife; 6-, 10-, and 12-inch taping blades; corner taping tool; pole sander or hand sander; tin snips

Just three coats of drywall compound with sanding result in smooth walls for a professional drywaller. But as a beginner, don't be surprised if it takes you four or five coats. Unless you have large holes that require patching plaster, use ready-mixed drywall joint compound. Dry-mix compounds provide more strength for trouble areas, but you need to work fast. To hide imperfections, apply texture to your walls with a rented texture gun and hopper.

DRYWALL FINISHING TIPS

Apply self-sticking mesh tape onto drywall wherever a tapered edge meets a tapered edge, as shown below right. Use paper tape everywhere else. The mesh tape requires less joint compound but does not work as well for inside corners.

Rusty, gunked-up tools ruin your work. Scrape, wash, and dry blades after every use.

When sanding, control the fine dust by using a fan to pull it out a window. Seal doorways and wear a breathing mask.

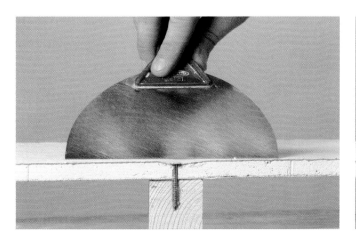

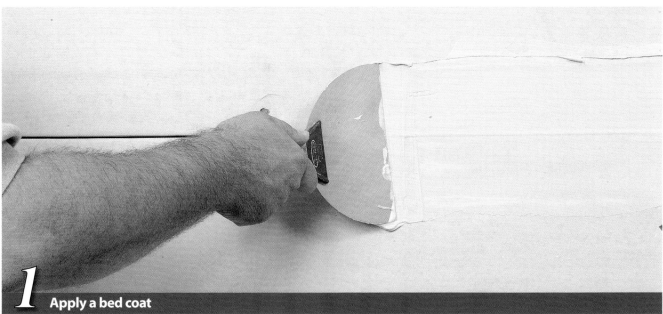

1 Apply a bed coat

Conceal nailheads by applying compound to a 6-inch taping blade and passing over the spot twice. Make sure you leave compound only in the depression and not on the rest of the sheet. Do this with each coat until the dimple is filled in completely. Joints are more difficult, especially butt joints. If you are using self-sticking mesh tape, simply cut pieces to fit, press them into place, and begin applying joint compound. For paper tape, start by spreading a bed coat over the joint with a 6-inch taping blade. Apply just enough compound to adhere to the paper tape. The photo at top right shows edges making a joint; a nail dimple is shown top left.

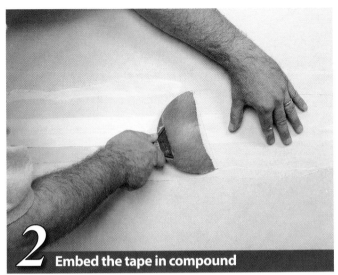

2 Embed the tape in compound

(Skip this step if you are using mesh tape.) Immediately after applying the bed coat to a joint, center a length of paper tape over the joint and press the tape firmly against the filled joint by running your taping blade along it. If the tape begins to slide, hold it in place with your hand. If bubbles form under the tape, if there are places where the tape is not sticking to the bed coat, or if wrinkles appear, peel the tape back and apply more compound. Then press the tape back.

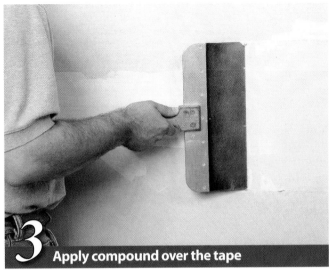

3 Apply compound over the tape

Load a 10-inch taping blade with compound and apply a smooth coat over the tape. Where two tapered edges meet, make sure the blade extends past both tapers. Fill in the tapers only so you have a flat wall surface. For butt joints, feather out the compound 7 to 9 inches on each side; a small ridge in the middle can be sanded later. After the compound dries, scrape off ridges and bumps, and sand. Apply and sand successive coats until the surface is smooth.

4 Coat outside corners

To protect and conceal drywall edges that meet at an outside corner, cut a piece of metal corner bead using tin snips. Fit the strip over the corner and fasten it to the wall, one side at a time. Drive nails or screws at 10-inch intervals. Make sure the flange of the corner bead does not protrude above what will be the finished surface by running a taping blade along the length of the corner bead. Fasten down any areas of flange that protrude. Apply a coat of joint compound with a 6-inch blade angled away from the corner. Allow one side of the blade to ride on the bead, the other side on the wall. For subsequent coats, use 10- and 12-inch blades.

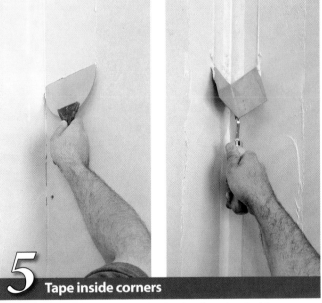

5 Tape inside corners

Apply a bed coat of compound to both sides of an inside corner with a 6-inch blade. Cut a piece of paper tape to the correct length, fold it, and position it by hand. Keep it straight to avoid wrinkles. Run a corner taping tool along its length to embed the tape in the compound. Lift and reapply compound wherever the tape has wrinkles, bubbles, or nonadhering spots.

Once the tape is embedded, apply some compound to the walls and some to the corner tool. Stroke on a smooth coat. This will take several passes and some practice. You may find it easier to feather out the edges with a 10-inch taping blade.

Roughing in an opening

If you plan to install a door in your wall, determine the rough opening dimensions you need. For a prehung door, measure the outside dimensions of the jamb, and add ½ inch for shimming. With a slab door (one that is not prehung), measure the width of the door, add 2½ inches for the side jambs and shims, and add 2 inches to the height for the head jamb, shims, and flooring. Standard door widths are 24, 26, 28, 30, 32, and 36 inches. Doors are usually 80 inches tall.

Once you know the opening size, build the wall as described on pages 60–67, with the addition of the framing members shown below. Each has a special function.

Jack studs are the vertical 2×4s on each side of the door opening. They are attached to a king stud or another jack stud. This doubling of studs provides solid, unbending support for the door.

The header is made of two 2×6s with a ½-inch plywood spacer sandwiched in between. (The plywood is needed to make the header 3½ inches thick, the same thickness as the wall framing.) The header rests on top of the jack studs and spans the top of the opening, supporting overhead loads. For openings that are less than 3 feet wide, you can use 2×4s instead of 2×6s.

Cripples are the short 2×4s added between the header and the top plate. They maintain a 16-inch on-center stud spacing for nailing drywall and help distribute the weight equally.

A window opening is like a door opening. You install a sill at the bottom of the window and add cripples between it and the wall's bottom plate.

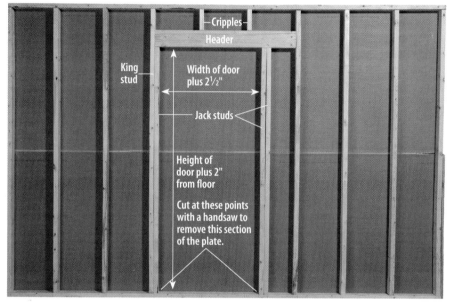

Cripples
Header
King stud
Width of door plus 2½"
Jack studs
Height of door plus 2" from floor
Cut at these points with a handsaw to remove this section of the plate.

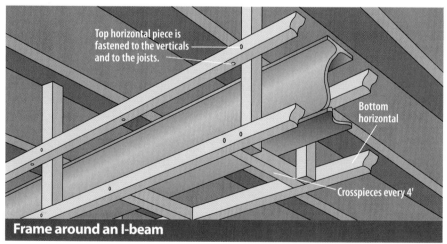

Top horizontal piece is fastened to the verticals and to the joists.
Bottom horizontal
Crosspieces every 4'

Frame around an I-beam

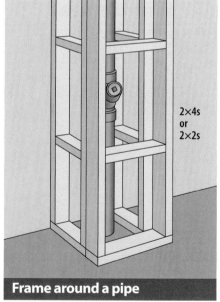

2×4s or 2×2s

Frame around a pipe

Use 2×2s to frame around a narrow obstruction such as a beam. Fasten the frame together with screws rather than nails because the structure is wobbly as you work. Drill pilot holes whenever you drive a screw near the end of a board. Make chalklines on the joists 1⅝ inches out from either side of the beam. On every other joist, attach a vertical 2×2, cutting it to extend 1¾ inches below the bottom of the beam. Fasten horizontal pieces to the bottom ends of the verticals, then fasten horizontal pieces at the top, driving screws into the vertical supports and the joists. Finish the framing by installing horizontal crosspieces about every 4 feet between the bottom horizontal members.

You can cover a soil stack or other tall, narrow obstruction with a frame. Mark lines on the floor and measure for top and bottom plates as you would for a regular wall. Draw plumb lines on the wall to use as guides. Build three narrow walls of 2×4s or 2×2s; raise them into position; and fasten them to the floor, ceiling, wall, and each other.

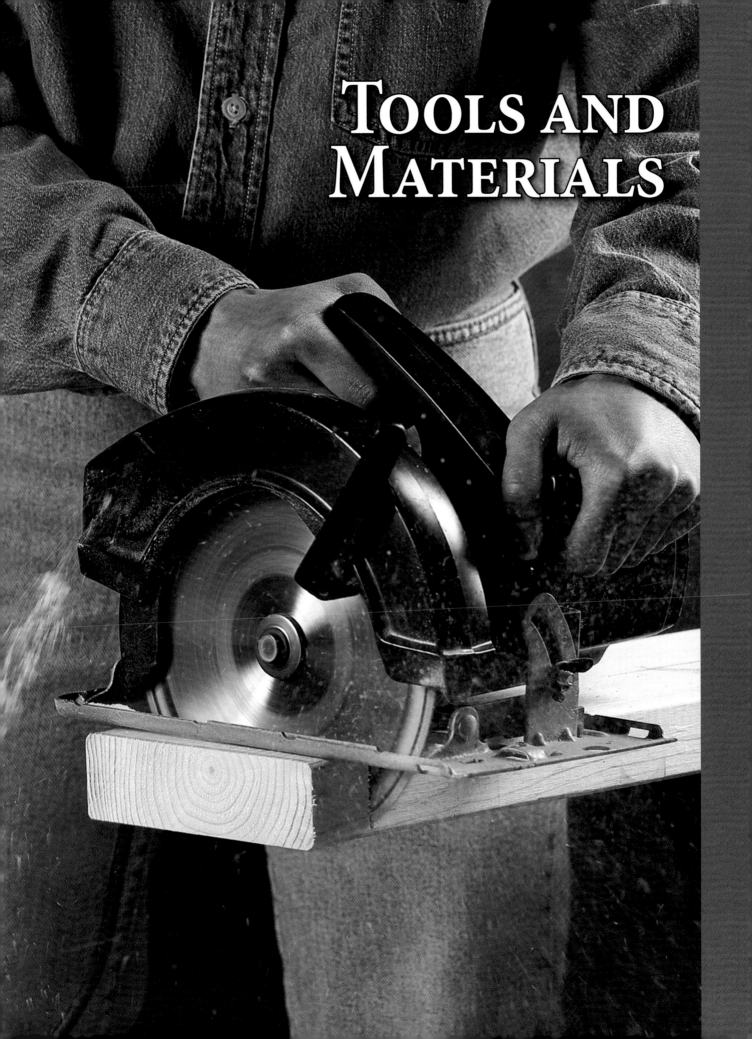

TOOLS AND MATERIALS

Selecting hand tools

The right hand tool makes your job easier and yields better results. Hand tools are relatively inexpensive, so it's easy to gather a collection. To avoid filling the basement with tools that you'll never use, assemble a basic tool kit and add to your collection when a job requires a new tool.

Typically the top-of-the-line contractor-type tool is of higher quality than an average homeowner needs, but inexpensive tools do not perform well. Your best choice is a midpriced model. If you need a tool to complete an unusual task and probably won't need it very often, consider renting it. If you buy it, purchase a less expensive version.

Adjustable clamp
Clamps parts that are too big for a C-clamp (below); sometimes called a bar clamp.

Adjustable wrench
Tightens nuts, bolts, and lag screws.

Awl
Marks and makes pilot holes for small screws.

Backsaw and miter box
Makes miter cuts. Consider a power mitersaw if you will make many cuts.

C-clamp
Holds parts together. Have an assortment of sizes handy.

Carpenter's level
Plumbs and levels large and small projects. A 2- or 4-foot model is good for most projects.

Cat's paw (nail puller)
Pulls nails easily, although it damages the wood (see page 40). Indispensable for demolition.

Caulking gun
Applies caulk, sealants, or construction adhesive from tubes.

Chalkline
Snaps long, straight lines. A chalkline also can double as a plumb bob.

Combination square
Checks 45- and 90-degree angles and lays out cutting lines (see pages 11 and 13).

Coping saw
Cuts intricate curves in thin materials.

Drywall saw
Cuts holes in drywall.

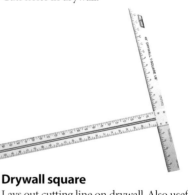

Drywall square
Lays out cutting line on drywall. Also useful for marking cutlines on plywood.

Hammer
Drives nails. The most popular model weighs 16 ounces and has curved claws. You'll find a variety of specialty hammers, including framing and wallboard hammers.

Locking pliers
Grip tightly for pulling nails.

Nail set
Sinks the heads of finishing nails below the surface of the work.

Drywall taping knives
Spread compound for taping drywall and patching damaged walls. Get 6-, 8-, and 12-inch blades to tape or patch almost any surface.

Handsaw
Crosscuts boards. Buy a small model that fits into a toolbox.

Plane
Shaves wood along the length of a board; use a plane to achieve the smoothest cut.

Flat pry bar
Pries off fastened lumber pieces with minimal damage to the wood. It also is handy for levering heavy objects into place (for example, reattaching a door to its hinges).

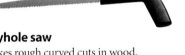

Keyhole saw
Makes rough curved cuts in wood.

Lineman's pliers
Enable you to grab items tightly from the front rather than the side of the tool.

Plumb bob
Establishes true vertical lines.

Framing square
Checks corners for square and aids in layout.

Pole sander
Sands large wall and ceiling areas easily. Buy a smaller sanding block for detail work (see page 55).

Rasp or wood file
Shapes wood.

Screwdrivers
Have various sizes of both phillips-tip and straight-tipped types on hand or buy a combination screwdriver that has four tips.

Side-cutting pliers
Useful for grabbing the pointed ends of finishing nails to pull them out of the back of molding without marring the face.

Layout square
Lays out 90- and 45-degree angle cuts quickly. Holds its shape after getting banged around. It slips into your back pocket and is handy for quickly marking cutlines on planks and framing material.

Spring clamp
Clamps thin materials that might be marred by a C-clamp (see page 76) or adjustable clamp (see pages 42–43 for other specialized clamps).

Staple gun
Attaches sheets of plastic or felt or installs fiberglass insulation.

Surface-forming tool
Substitutes for a plane but does not cut as straight or as smooth. It is more versatile, however, and comes in handy for fine-tuning anything from foamboard to wallboard.

T-bevel
Set this adjustable gauge to the angle between two surfaces and you can mark the angle on another piece of material.

Tape measure
Measures almost anything. Buy a 25-foot one with a 1-inch-wide blade; this extends farther and lasts longer than a ¾-inch one.

Groove-joint pliers
Grabs almost anything firmly and works well for pulling nails.

Utility knife
Cuts and marks in many situations. Most people prefer one with a retractable blade.

Wood chisel
Pares wood to shape mortises and makes rough notches in places where a saw doesn't reach. Choose chisels with plastic or metal-capped handles for durability.

Basic power tools

A circular saw, a cordless drill/ driver, a jigsaw (sometimes called a saber saw), and a power drill are musts for your basic toolkit. With the two saws you can make straight and curved cuts quickly in almost any material. The drills help you make holes of almost any size and drive screws quickly and easily. With these four tools you can handle almost any household carpentry job.

Circular saw

A circular saw crosscuts, angle-cuts, rips (cuts lengthwise), and even bevels lumber easily and cleanly. Don't worry if the saw has a plastic housing; many plastics are very strong. Do look at the metal baseplate. A baseplate made of thin, stamped metal can warp; look for a thicker base made of extruded or cast metal. A saw that takes $7^1/_4$-inch blades is the usual choice. It allows you to cut to a depth of about $2^1/_2$ inches at 90 degrees and to cut through a piece of 2× lumber even when the blade is set at 45 degrees.

Horsepower is not important when choosing a circular saw. Instead look at the amperage and the type of bearings. A low-cost saw pulls only 9 or 10 amps and usually has sleeve bearings. This means less power, a shorter life because it heats up easily, and less-precise cuts because the blade may wobble somewhat. Better saws are rated at 12 or 13 amps and often have ball bearings. This combination of extra power and smoother operation makes for long life and accurate cutting. Worm-drive saws are heavy and relatively expensive. As is often the case, a midpriced saw is your best choice.

Jigsaw

When buying a jigsaw, examine the baseplate and the mechanism for adjusting it. On less-expensive saws, these are flimsy and eventually wobble, making it difficult to keep the blade aligned vertically. Variable speed is a useful option. A saw that draws 3 amps or more handles most cutting jobs.

Power drill

Be sure to get a variable-speed, reversible power drill. Unless you will be doing heavy-duty work, you don't need one with a $1/_2$-inch chuck; a $3/_8$-inch one is fine. Buy a drill that pulls at least 3.5 amps. A keyless chuck simplifies changing bits, but some people prefer a keyed chuck for a tighter grip on the bit.

Cordless drill/driver

A cordless drill/driver frees you to work without the mess of electrical cords. Buy one rated at least 9.6 volts, preferably more. If possible, get an extra battery pack so you won't have to wait for a battery to charge.

Specialized power tools

The more carpentry jobs you take on, the more power tools you will need or want to own. Many of these are high-priced items, so research carefully before making a purchase. If you will return often to a particular tool, pay extra to get a high-quality tool that lasts.

If you will use it only rarely, settle for a lesser-quality tool.

To determine the quality of a tool, check the amperage rather than the horsepower. Compare models and avoid buying the one with the lowest amperage rating. A plastic housing is

not necessarily a sign of poor quality. But do check mechanisms and metal attachments to see if they're solid. A tool with ball bearings runs smoother and lasts longer than one with other types of bearings.

Belt sander
Quickly sands large areas. Make sure it uses belts that are easily available—3×24 inches is the most common size. A good belt sander is fairly heavy and has a large dust collector. You can switch from rough to fine sanding belts; however, because it is difficult to handle for fine work, you may find you will want to use another method for the final sanding.

Biscuit joiner
Cuts slots for joint biscuits. If you plan a project that calls for joining two pieces of lumber side by side, this tool produces professional-looking results with ease (see page 50).

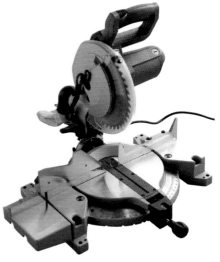

Power mitersaw
Crosscuts or miter-cuts boards and molding. This tool (also called a chopsaw or cutoff saw) resembles a circular saw mounted onto a pivot assembly. It makes quick, precise crosscuts and miter cuts. Make sure you get a saw large enough to cut all the way through the stock you want to cut; a 10-inch blade handles most projects. A sliding compound mitersaw offers the greatest versatility.

Bench grinder
Sharpens tools and shapes metal objects. Bolt it to your workbench and it's ready to use at a moment's notice.

Drill press
Drills holes precisely. You can purchase a drill press or a drill stand that uses a regular power drill. A stand is less expensive than a drill press but takes more time to set up and use.

Random-orbit sander
Sands for finishing. It works by moving rapidly in overlapping orbits. Some people prefer the finish of an older-style orbital sander, which moves in an elliptical pattern . Some units switch from orbital to a nearly straight action.

Router

Forms a wide variety of decorative or joinery profiles on lumber. Routers are either fixed-base models, which are ideal for edge work, or plunge routers. The head of a plunge router moves up and down on the base, so you can start routing anywhere on a board.

Reciprocating saw

Makes quick, rough cuts in places no other saw will reach. You'll want a reciprocating saw for demolition and extensive remodeling work. If you need to remove portions of walls or floors, this tool can save you a lot of time and frustration.

Radial arm saw

A general-purpose power saw. It is best suited to crosscuts, but it can make rip cuts too. A sliding compound mitersaw often saws miters and crosscuts more accurately, and a tablesaw is more convenient for rip cuts.

Tablesaw

Makes precise, straight cuts. Use it for dado cuts as well. It also works for crosscuts and miter cuts (see page 27), but not as easily as a power mitersaw. Choose a model that has a solid table that will not wiggle as you work on it, a fence that stays firmly in place, and a powerful motor. You need a lot of room in your shop if you cut sheets of plywood or long pieces of lumber on a tablesaw.

TOOL SAFETY TIPS

Safety is the result of following guidelines and exercising common sense. Just one moment's lapse of concentration when working with a power tool can lead to serious injury. To minimize risks, keep the following guidelines in mind:

- Use tools only for the jobs they were designed to do. If an instruction manual came with the tool, take the time to read it to find out what the tool will do and what it will not do.
- Check on the condition of a tool before using it. A dull cutting edge or a loose-fitting hammerhead, for example, spells trouble. Also inspect the cord of a power tool to make sure it's not damaged.
- Don't work with tools if you're tired or in a hurry.
- Don't work with tools if you have recently been drinking alcohol.
- Wear goggles whenever the operation you are performing could result in eye injury.
- The safety mechanisms on power tools are for your protection. Don't tamper with or remove them.
- Don't wear loose-fitting clothes or dangling jewelry while you are using tools.
- Keep people, especially children, at a safe distance while you're using any tool. Before you let children use a tool, instruct them on how to operate it and supervise them as they work.
- Before servicing or adjusting a power tool, unplug it and allow moving parts to stop.

Organize your tools

If you're serious about doing carpentry work around your house, you need a convenient, comfortable, well-organized place to work and store the tools and materials you accumulate. Your carpentry headquarters can be a full-fledged shop, or it may be a simple workbench and a corner set aside for lumber. But you need a work center—and the sooner, the better.

You can build your workshop in a basement, garage, seldom-used room, or even a closet or attic. A basement has several advantages. It's off the beaten path, so you needn't worry about disrupting family activities as you work. In most homes it's also one of the few areas with a sizable amount of unused space—an important factor if you want to use stationary power tools. However, if your basement tends to get wet or if it's difficult to get sheet goods into it, you may want to investigate other areas.

Once you've decided on the tools you would like to have, plan your space carefully. Here are some tips:

■ Make sure there is plenty of light. Large fluorescent fixtures usually work best. Make sure the lights are positioned so you won't accidentally bump the bulbs.

■ To provide power for your heavy-duty tools, run at least one 20-amp electrical circuit with a ground fault circuit interrupter to the shop. Large shops should have separate circuits for tools and lights. Position electrical outlets strategically around the workshop so power is never far away.

■ Give yourself a way to easily carry your tools from place to place. An apron made to fit a 5-gallon bucket has room for a drill, power cord, and other large tools in the middle and smaller tools in pockets around the outside. You may prefer a toolbox for smaller items.

■ Have at least two sawhorses on hand. Use these to support bulky sheet goods and lengths of lumber while you work on them in the shop and to help you work at job sites.

■ Make it as easy as possible to keep your shop clean, or have a broom, dustpan, and portable vacuum on hand. If you do a lot of woodworking, buy a dust collector—a central vacuum with tubes running to stationary tools. Have large garbage containers you can easily carry out to the trash.

■ If you have a forced-air furnace, make sure the dust you make cannot get sucked into it. Change the filters often.

■ Make sure the work area has adequate ventilation. If possible, install an exhaust fan that can change the air in the shop every four minutes. The cubic feet (length times width times height) in your shop determines the size of the fan needed.

Well-planned workshop

This well-designed workshop makes it a pleasure to complete virtually any project. The ideal workshop should contain ample bright light and grounded electrical outlets throughout the room and along the workbenches to avoid extension cords. Plan to include wall-mounted and enclosed storage for equipment and materials, workbenches, and easy-to-clean, soft floor mats of a durable material such as rubber or vinyl.

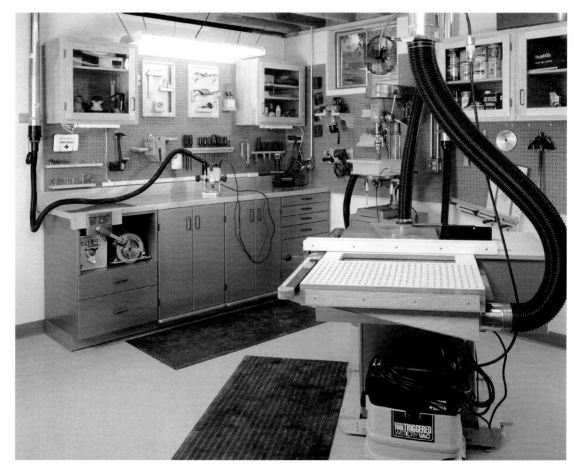

■ The workbench is the activity hub of every shop. A full-size workbench typically measures 6 to 8 feet long, 24 to 36 inches deep, and 40 to 42 inches high. You may want to make it the exact height of your tablesaw or radial arm saw. This makes it easy to handle sheets of plywood for cutting, using the bench as an additional cutting support. If you have limited space, it may make sense to have a smaller bench on wheels so you can store it out of the way. You may want to include a storage shelf below the workbench surface area. See pages 100–101 for how to build a workbench.

■ Attach a sheet of perforated hardboard to the wall near your workbench for hanging tools. Install the board so it extends 1 or 2 inches out from the wall so tool hooks can be inserted. If the hooks tend to pop out every time you remove a tool, glue them in place with construction adhesive or hot glue.

■ Provide plenty of storage for your tools and materials. See page 93 for how to store lumber.

WORKSHOP ORGANIZERS

You need a good storage system if you want to store all your nails, screws, small tools, and various pieces of hardware so they are easy to find. In addition to ready-made organizers, consider these possibilities:

■ Nail glass jar lids to an overhead surface so you can reach up and unscrew jars full of fasteners or hardware. The great advantage here is that you can see what's inside each container.

■ Keep items visible. Use open shelves or place the shelves at eye level so it's easy to find items you've stored.

Keep your tools organized
Many options are available for organizing tools and materials. Tool pouches or belts let you carry tools with you as you work on a project, eliminating the need to interrupt your work to get items you forgot. Keep tools in the same pockets all the time so you'll always reach for the right tool. Tool bags allow you to tote all of the tools you need to your work area but free you from the constant weight of a tool pouch or belt. Side pockets store smaller, frequently used items such as hammers and screwdrivers. The main compartment is large enough to comfortably house a power tool in addition to larger hand tools. Plastic organizer cases are great for storing hardware and fasteners in separate compartments. These cases are ideal for holding small numbers of numerous materials rather than nails by the pound necessary for a big job.

Selecting and buying lumber

As you learn carpentry techniques, it's important to become familiar with the characteristics and uses of various types of lumber and how to choose the wood that works best for a particular project.

There are two basic types of lumber: softwoods, from coniferous trees, and hardwoods, from deciduous trees. Wood is graded according to how many knots it has and the quality of its surface. (See the chart below for the most common grades.) Some lumberyards have their own grading systems, but they usually simply rename these standard grades.

No matter what species of lumber you buy, look out for the wood problems shown at right. Generally a board that is heavily twisted, bowed,

cupped, or crooked is not usable, although some bowed boards will lie down as you nail them into place. Knots are only a cosmetic problem unless they are loose and likely to pop out. Checking, which is a rift in the surface, also is only cosmetic. Splits cannot be repaired and widen in time. Cut split ends off.

The nominal dimensions of wood are used when ordering lumber. Keep in mind that the actual dimensions of the lumber are smaller (see the chart on the oppoosite page). Large quantities of lumber sometimes are figured by the board foot. A board foot is the equivalent of a piece 12 inches square and 1 inch thick (see chart below). Most lumberyards don't require you to figure board feet.

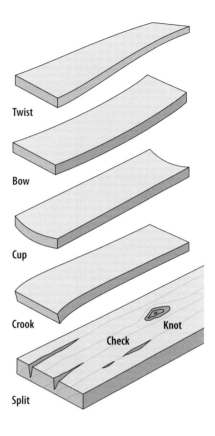

Twist

Bow

Cup

Crook

Split

Check

Knot

COMMON GRADES OF WOOD	
Grade	**Characteristics**
Clear	Has no knots.
Select or select structural	Very high-quality wood. Broken down into Nos. 1–3 or grades A–D; the lower grades have more knots.
No. 2 common	Has tight knots, no major blemishes; good for shelving.
No. 3 common	Knots may be loose; often blemished or damaged.
Construction or standard	Good strength; used for general framing.
Utility	Economy grade; used for rough framing.

INSPECT BEFORE BUYING

If you order lumber by telephone, you get someone else's choice of boards, not yours. Lumberyards usually have plenty of substandard wood lying around. The only way to be sure you do not get some of it is to pick out the boards yourself. Some lumberyards don't allow you to sort through the stacks because they want to keep wood neatly stacked—the only way to keep lumber from warping. But they should at least let you stand by and approve the selection. Failing that, confirm that you can return boards that are substandard.

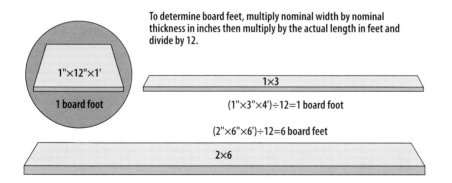

To determine board feet, multiply nominal width by nominal thickness in inches then multiply by the actual length in feet and divide by 12.

1"×12"×1'

1 board foot

1×3

(1"×3"×4')÷12=1 board foot

(2"×6"×6')÷12=6 board feet

2×6

Type		Description and Uses	Nominal Sizes	Actual Sizes
Furring		Rough wood of small dimensions. For furring drywall and paneling, interior and exterior trim, shimming, stakes, crates, light-duty frames, latticework, and edging.	1×2 1×3	$3/4×1^1/_2$ $3/4×2^1/_2$
Finish lumber		Smooth-finished lumber. For paneling, trim, shelving, light framing, structural finishing, forming, siding, decking, casing, valances, cabinets, built-ins, and furniture.	1×4 1×6 1×8 1×10 1×12	$3/4×3^1/_2$ $3/4×5^1/_2$ $3/4×7^1/_4$ $3/4×9^1/_4$ $3/4×11^1/_4$
Tongue-and-groove		Tongues and grooves connect into each other for a tight fit. For decorative interior wall treatments, exterior siding, flooring, and subflooring.	1×4 1×6 1×8	Actual sizes vary from mill to mill.
Shiplap		One edge fits on top of the other. For decorative wall treatments, siding, decking, exterior sheathing, and subflooring.	1×4 1×6 1×8	$3/4×3^1/_8$ $3/4×5^1/_8$ $3/4×6^7/_8$
Dimensional lumber		Studs are usually 2×4, sometimes 2×6. Planks are 6 or more inches wide. For structural framing (wall studs, ceiling and floor joists, rafters, headers, top and bottom plates), structural finishing, forming, exterior decking and fencing, and stair components (stringers, steps).	2×2 2×3 2×4 2×6 2×8 2×10 2×12 4×4 4×6 6×6	$1^1/_2×1^1/_2$ $1^1/_2×2^1/_2$ $1^1/_2×3^1/_2$ $1^1/_2×5^1/_2$ $1^1/_2×7^1/_4$ $1^1/_2×9^1/_4$ $1^1/_2×11^1/_4$ $3^1/_2×3^1/_2$ $3^1/_2×5^1/_2$ $5^1/_2×5^1/_2$
Glue-laminate		Layers of dimensional lumber laid flat on top of each other and laminated into one solid piece. Used for rafters, joists, and beams. Can be stained for exposed beams.	4×10 4×12 6×10 6×12	$3^1/_2×9$ $3^1/_2×12$ $5^1/_2×9$ $5^1/_2×12$
Microlaminate		Veneers glued together with crossing grains like plywood, only thicker. For rafters, joists, and beams.	4×12	$3^1/_2×11^3/_8$

Selecting wood

Just as you spend time considering a new wall paint color to update a room, you should take time to investigate your options before selecting wood for your carpentry or woodworking project. Each type of wood has its own characteristics. These characteristics influence how you work with the wood and the finished appearance of the project. Before you make a trip to the local lumberyard or home improvement center, understand the basic characteristics and common uses of common wood species.

The first distinction is softwood vs. hardwood. This is determined by the tree the wood comes from rather than its physical hardness or softness. Hardwoods come from deciduous trees—those with leaves—and softwoods come from conifers—evergreen trees.

In part, the selection of wood for a project should be based on whether the wood is suitable for a particular use. For example, pine is relatively soft and weak, so it is not a good choice for a bookcase to house a comprehensive collection of literary classics. Oak, which is much stronger, may be the perfect choice.

Your choice of wood, however, also should involve aesthetics. Oak may prove to be an excellent choice for strong, sturdy bookcases, but you may not care for its open grain. You may opt for maple, cherry, or walnut instead. Following are some specific items to consider as you choose the ideal wood for your project.

Consider the wood's resistance to dents and scratches. Selecting a softwood or hardwood that has a relatively soft or medium hardness probably does not make sense for a high-traffic area or a location that takes a lot of abuse, such as a countertop or cutting block. Maple, for example, is among the hardest of domestic woods—you may

even have heard it referred to as "hard maple" or "rock maple." That's why most chopping blocks are maple.

Some wood species are said to have better "workability" than others. This means you'll find them easier to saw, chisel, plane, or drive screws into. In general, softer woods are easier to work with than harder woods, but workability can vary greatly from board to board. Straight-grained boards are much easier to work with than boards that have lots of knots or wild swirling grain. Of course wild grain also can add lots of visual interest.

Consider the grade of wood, no matter the species. (See page 84 for information about the most common grades of wood.) Using wood free from defects may not be important for all projects. For example, unfinished basement storage shelves require sound wood, but not knot-free wood. Some defects can even add aesthetic value to a finished project. A knot might give the touch of rustic character you want for a door in a country-theme interior. Other projects—such as a showpiece cabinet finished with a natural stain and installed in a main living area—require a top grade of wood.

Look at the selection of wood available at a local lumberyard. The colors, grains, and textures of the various woods can have an impact on the overall look of your project. For most projects it's best to avoid wood with numerous knots, pitch streaks, splits, checks, and stains. Even for a rustic project, you should avoid wood that is heavily twisted, bowed, cupped, or crooked.

The stability of wood determines its tendency to shrink and warp. Wood for interior construction typically has a moisture content of 6 to 8 percent. But the moisture content of the air (humidity) may be significantly higher, causing significant shrinking and warping that over time can undermine the success of your project. Check with the supplier of the wood. Remember that even properly dried wood shrinks and swells in response to seasonal changes of humidity and temperature.

Finishes don't completely stop moisture exchange, but they do reduce

the amount of moisture that moves through the wood, thus making it more stable. Heavy hardwoods respond more to changes in humidity and temperature than lighter woods.

Most hardwoods are too dense to drive screws or nails into without predrilling. You can find out with a test using a piece of scrap lumber to determine whether you need to predrill holes to avoid splitting and cracking the wood, and to avoid bending or breaking the fasteners. (See page 37 for more information about pilot holes.)

No matter what type and grade of wood you select, always sand wood before finishing to provide a smooth surface. Sand with the grain, never across. Start with a coarse-grit sandpaper and slowly work toward a fine grit that provides a smooth surface. (For more tips on sanding, see page 55.) Even wood that is to be painted needs sanding with medium-grit sandpaper to remove "mill marks"—ripples caused by the machine that planed the wood to size.

PRO TIPS AND TERMS

Use this information from carpentry and woodworking pros to help you select and purchase wood for your next project.

- ■ The price for a given species of wood may vary greatly by region. Local woods usually are less expensive than species that need to be shipped from distant places. You'll pay significantly less for redwood in California than you will in Pennsylvania. But Pennsylvanians are more likely to find a good price for black cherry, which is abundant in eastern forests.
- ■ You can select for grain and then stain. If, for example, your heart but not your checkbook is set on cherry, take a look at birch. The grain and hardness are very similar. With the right stain, you can achieve the cherry look you're after.
- ■ Quartersawn lumber is less likely to warp than plain-sawn wood. To tell the difference, look at the end of the board: Quartersawn boards have growth rings that are fairly straight and roughly perpendicular to the faces. A plainsawn board has rings that curve toward one face of the board. Unfortunately quartersawing yields much less usable lumber from a log, so quartersawn boards are costlier.
- ■ Hardwood lumber thickness is always specified in quarters of an inch. So you don't buy a 2× oak board. Instead you buy 8/4 (eight-quarter) oak, which is actually $1\frac{3}{4}$ inches thick after surfacing and drying. Hardwood boards are most likely to be random lengths and widths rather than standard lumber sizes.
- ■ Hardwood lumber is sold by the board foot. This is any volume equal to 1 foot by 1 foot by 1 inch (see page 84).

SOFTWOOD SELECTOR

Species	Characteristics	Common uses
Cedar, cypress	Similar to redwood—only the heartwood is resistant to rot. Weak, brittle; resists warping; pleasant aroma; easy to work.	Siding, paneling, rough trim, roof shingles and shakes, decks.
Fir	Heavy, very strong, hard; holds nails well; good resistance to warping and shrinkage; somewhat difficult to work.	Framing studs, joists, posts, and beams; flooring; subflooring.
Hem/fir	A general classification that takes in a variety of species, including hemlock and fir. Lightweight, soft, fairly strong; warps easily; may shrink; easy to work.	Framing, exterior fascia, flooring, subflooring, trim.
Pine	From eastern, northern, and western trees. Lightweight, soft, fairly weak; good resistance to warping but with a tendency to shrink; easy to work.	Paneling, trim (molding), flooring, cabinets.
Redwood	Durable and resistant to rot and insects in the heartwood. Light, soft, not as strong as fir or Southern pine; tendency to split; easy to work.	Exterior posts and beams, siding, paneling, decks, fences.
Southern pine	Very hard, stiff, excellent strength; holds nails well; has a tendency to crack, splinter, warp; works with average ease.	Framing, subflooring.
Spruce	Lightweight, soft, fairly strong; resistant to splitting and warping; easy to work.	Framing, flooring, subflooring, trim (molding).
Treated lumber	Several species can be treated—most often fir, hem/fir, and Southern pine are used. Green or brown color fades in time, leaving the wood a dirty gray; extremely resistant to rot and insects. Workability depends on species.	Bottom framing plates that rest on concrete; other framing that might come into contact with water; decks; fences.

To protect your wood project and enhance its beauty, complete your work by applying the right finish. Clear finishes that enhance the natural beauty of wood and stains to color the wood are available. If painting, select a high-quality paint that resists abrasion and denting while being washable for easy cleaning. (See page 57 for information about filling and finishing your projects.)

Softwoods

Unless you're installing major structural components that will bear significant weight, such as floor or ceiling joists, you can't make a serious mistake when buying softwoods. In most cases you simply want to buy the wood that looks best or is the least expensive.

Softwood usually is less expensive than hardwood because it comes from trees that grow faster. In general,

the disadvantage of softwood is evident in its name: most are soft, although Douglas fir is as hard as most hardwoods. If you use softwood for furniture and other objects that get handled and bumped, plan on seeing some dents in it after time.

Most retail suppliers stock only a few species of softwood. The chart on page 87 summarizes the chief characteristics of each. In most cases you'll be choosing between grades of lumber rather than species. Which grade you choose depends on the nature of your project.

Softwood grading is difficult because several grading systems exist. Most often, however, you'll find two general classifications: select and common.

Use select lumber, which comes in several subgrades, for trim or cabinetry where finished appearance counts. For all other projects, common lumber

does nicely. Common lumber is graded as No. 1, No. 2, and No. 3.

With some lumber suppliers, you can dispense with the grades and talk about more straightforward characteristics such as "clear" (without knots) and "tight-knot" (having only small knots without cracks).

Of course, the better the grade—that is, the fewer the defects—the more you pay for the product. Often, however, a better grade is only slightly more expensive. Once you gain some experience, you will be able to sort through the lumber rack carefully and find pieces that are at the top of their classes—for instance, a piece of No. 2 common that looks as if it could have been classified as select.

HARDNESS OF SELECTED WOODS		
Softwoods		
Soft	**Medium**	**Hard**
Western red cedar	Pine White fir	Douglas fir
Hardwoods		
Soft	**Medium**	**Hard**
Poplar Basswood Willow	Black ash Cherry Paper birch Silver maple	Black walnut Red, white oak Yellow birch White ash

Creative wood sources

If your basic carpentry pursuits lead you to more serious woodworking projects, one potential source for wood is trees downed by a storm. Make sure you receive permission from the homeowners or local officials. The wood from a tree such as this would have to be milled and dried before use.

HARDWOOD SELECTOR

Species	Characteristics	Common Uses
Birch	Hard, strong; fine-grained; resists shrinking and warping; holds paint well. Similar in color to maple—sometimes used as a more economical replacement. Finishes fairly well; hard to cut.	Paintable cabinets, paneling, trim, furniture.
Mahogany	Durable; fine-grained; resistant to shrinking, warping, and swelling. Finishes well; easy to cut. (Not to be confused with lauan mahogany, a less-expensive material that is used for veneers and plywoods.)	Fine furniture, cabinets, millwork, veneers.
Maple	Extremely hard, strong; pieces with bird's-eye or wavy grains are highly prized. Color ranges from reddish to nearly white. Finishes well; hard to cut.	Flooring (basketball and bowling alley floors are made of maple), butcher blocks, veneers, countertops, millwork, and molding.
Poplar	Lightweight, soft texture; fine-grained. White to yellow-brown in color. Paints well; easy to cut.	Paintable furniture, cabinets, trim, paneling, places where a less-expensive hardwood will do.
Red oak	Hard, strong, rigid; pronounced, open grain; resists warping but may shrink if not well dried. Reddish color. Finishes well; moderately hard to cut.	Flooring, doors, furniture, cabinets, molding, stair rails.
Walnut	Hard, heavy, extra strong; fairly pronounced, straight grain; resists warping and shrinking. Light to dark brown in color. Finishes well; cuts fairly easily.	Fine furniture, cabinets, millwork, paneling, inlays, veneers.
White oak	Hard, strong; open grain but not as pronounced as red oak; resists shrinking and warping. Golden color. Finishes well; moderately hard to cut.	Better than red oak for flooring—less variation in color. Millwork, molding, furniture, cabinets, doors, stair rails, balusters.

Hardwoods

You can buy various types of plastic-laminated products made to look like hardwood, but there is no substitute for the real thing. Hardwood flooring and trim give a home elegance unmatched by any other product. For furniture and cabinetry, nothing quite measures up in appearance and durability.

Hardwood trees grow slowly, so prices tend to be higher than they are for softwood. But prices fluctuate widely from year to year, and often the difference is surprisingly small. Oak flooring, for example, sometimes costs less than softwood flooring.

The more expensive hardwoods are milled to make use of virtually every splinter of wood. Instead of the standard sizes, some hardwoods are sold in pieces of varying lengths and widths. Sometimes the boards are smooth-surfaced on only two sides (S2S), leaving the edges rough. Hardwoods may be priced by the board foot (see page 84).

Hardwood grading differs from that of softwoods. It is based primarily on the amount of clear surface area on the board. The best grade is FAS (firsts and seconds), which is the most knot-free. Select boards have defects on one side only; No. 1 common has tiny, tight knots; No. 2 common has larger knots.

Most lumberyards and home centers stock only a limited assortment of a few hardwood species. For the best selection, find local millers or stores that specialize in hardwoods. They stock or can order a wide selection of species. Some Internet dealers sell hardwood and exotic lumber in small quantities for home projects. Buy from a dealer you trust because you won't be able to pick your boards. Shipping is often costly too.

HARDWOOD FROM MANAGED FORESTS

Concerned that your lumber may come from irreplaceable forests? The Forest Stewardship Council is an international organization that promotes sustainable forestry and certifies producers who meet the group's standards. Find the council on the Internet at fscus.org.

Selecting moldings

All rooms use at least some molding, usually along the base of walls and around windows and doors. In those places, molding covers up gaps. Other molding protects corners from dents or protects walls from damage by chair backs.

In other places, such as around mantels, along the ceiling, and where paint and wallcoverings meet in the middle of a wall, molding serves a decorative function. The molding you choose helps define the look of a room.

Molding is available in random lengths from 6 to 16 feet. Most molding is softwood, usually pine. Some popular types are available in hardwood, usually oak, which is a little more expensive. Finger-jointed molding is made of short pieces joined end to end. It costs less than solid molding but is suitable only when you paint the moldings.

The cost of molding does add up, so make a list of each piece you need, rounding up the length to the nearest foot. Add 5 percent to allow for trimming and fitting. (See pages 111–116 for molding installation tips.)

ALTERNATIVE MATERIALS

Plastic molding is easy to work with but some has woodgrain finishes that may not suit your style. High-quality plastic moldings replicate elaborate crown moldings and plaster moldings. Some feature simplified installation systems that make the job easy.

If you plan to paint molding rather than stain it, save time and money with a preprimed molding.

Paper-covered hardboard molding is inexpensive but can be difficult to cut and install neatly, and the paper pattern can mar easily.

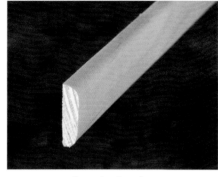

Screen bead regular

Screen bead fluted

Half round

Quarter round

Inside corner

Outside corner

Base shoe

Baseboard

Ranch stop

Colonial stop

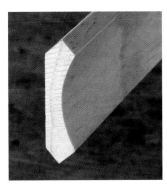

Cove molding

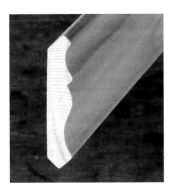

Crown molding

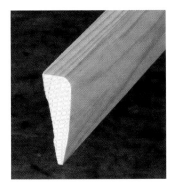

Ranch casing

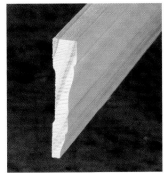

Colonial casing

Wainscot/ply cap

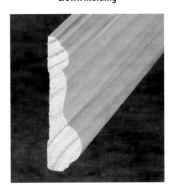

Chair rail

Batten

Brick mold

MOLDING SELECTOR

Common types	Typical uses
Screen bead: regular and fluted	Cover seams where screening fastens to frames; finish edges of shelves
Half round	Serves as screen bead, shelf edging, and lattice
Quarter round	General corner trim and inside corner guard
Inside corner and outside corner	Conceal seams and protect areas where walls meet at corners
Base shoe and baseboard	Trim and protect walls at their base
Stop: ranch and Colonial	Attach to door jambs to limit door swing; hold inside sash of windows in place
Cove and crown	Trim and conceal joints between walls and ceilings
Casing: ranch and Colonial	Both trim around interior windows and doors
Wainscot/ply cap	Conceals paneling edge; tops off wainscoting
Chair rail	Protects walls from chair backs; hides seams where wall materials meet
Batten	Conceals vertical and horizontal panel seams
Brick mold	Used with all types of exterior cladding (not just brick) to trim around doors and windows

Selecting sheet goods

Sheet goods are easy to work with and an inexpensive way to neatly cover large surface areas. For many applications, they provide the strength and appearance you need at a fraction of the cost of dimensional lumber.

Plywood is made by laminating thin layers (or plies) of wood using water-resistant glue. The plies are sandwiched, with the grain of each successive ply running at 90 degrees to the grain of the previous layer. This gives plywood its tremendous strength, as you find if you try to break a piece in two. The front and back surface plies may be made of softwood—usually fir—or hardwood. A plywood surface rated A is smooth and free of defects; B, C, and D faces are progressively rougher. Both faces need not be graded the same, for example, A-C. T1-11 plywood siding is made with exterior adhesive and a rough veneer.

Wood particles, sawdust, and glue are compressed and bonded together by heat to form **particleboard** and **hardboard**. This process produces a material that is hard but easy to break. Hardboard comes in tempered (very hard) and untempered (softer) composition and is available in a variety of textures. Particleboard comes in a variety of densities. Particleboard laminated with a plastic surface is handy for cabinet construction. **Waferboard** is made by a similar process but with scraps of thin wood rather than sawdust, making it similar to plywood.

Drywall, sometimes called wallboard, is made of gypsum powder sandwiched between layers of heavy paper. **Cement board**, used as a base for tile installations, is made with portland cement and fillers.

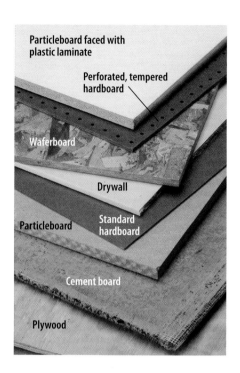

Particleboard faced with plastic laminate

Perforated, tempered hardboard

Waferboard

Drywall

Particleboard

Standard hardboard

Cement board

Plywood

SHEET GOODS SELECTOR

Material	Grades and Common Types	Thickness (in inches)	Common Panel Sizes (in feet)	Typical Uses
Plywood sheathing	C-D, C-D Exterior	$3/8, 1/2, 5/8, 3/4$	4×8	Sheathing, subflooring, underlayment, structural supports. Tongue-and-groove and shiplap versions are available.
Finish plywood	A-B, A-C, B-C	$1/4, 3/8, 1/2, 5/8, 3/4$	4×8, 2×4	Cabinets, cabinet doors, shelves, soffits.
Hardwood plywood	A-A (or A-2), G1S (good one side); hardwood side sometimes labeled N	$1/4, 3/4$	4×8, 2×4	Cabinets, cabinet doors, shelves, wall panels.
Lauan subflooring	Only one type	$1/4$	4×8, 2×4	Underlayment for vinyl tiles or sheet goods, backing for cabinets.
T1-11 siding	Rough, with grooves variously spaced	$3/8, 1/2, 5/8$	4×8, 4×9	Exterior siding.
Oriented-strand board	Only one type	$1/4, 7/16, 1/2, 3/4$	4×8	Roof sheathing, underlayment.
Particleboard	Density of material varies	$1/4, 3/8, 1/2, 5/8, 3/4$	4×8, 2×4	Underlayment, core material for laminated furniture and countertops.
Hardboard	Standard, tempered, perforated	$1/8, 1/4$	4×8, 2×4	Underlayment, drawer bottoms and partitions, cabinet backs, tool organizers.
Drywall	Standard, water-resistant greenboard	$1/4, 3/8, 1/2, 5/8$	4×8, 4×10, 4×12	Interior walls.
Cement board	Cement/clay, cement/foam	$5/16, 1/2$	32"×60"	Backing for wall tiles, underlayment for ceramic floors.

Handling and storing materials

One of the joys of having your own workshop is the pile of useful materials you collect over time. To ensure a safe, uneventful trip home from your home center, secure materials to your vehicle with rope, bungee cords, or twine. For large purchases or if your vehicle cannot handle the load, pay a little extra to rent a truck or have the materials delivered to your house.

When transporting or unloading sheet goods, have a helper on hand. If that's not possible, lift a panel with one hand near the center of each long edge, as shown below. Pick the panel up and rest it on your shoulder; avoid carrying it with a bent back. The exception is drywall: Because it's thin,

heavy, and brittle, it can snap under its own weight. Get help with drywall. Take care not to damage the edges or scratch the surface of the sheets.

Too quickly, however, your pile of material can become a headache and an eyesore. To keep boards and sheet goods easily accessible and to prevent warping and other damage, keep these tips in mind:

■ Store materials in a cool, dry place, off the floor. Moisture can distort lumber, delaminate some plywoods, and render drywall useless. If your basement gets wet occasionally, store materials above the high-water line.

■ Ideally sheet goods should be stored flat. Most people lack the room to do

this and stand sheet goods on edge, as shown below. Keep the sheets as vertical as possible to keep them from bowing.

■ Build a storage rack like the one shown below to keep lumber at eye level. You should see the ends of boards clearly and pull out what you need easily.

■ If you don't build a rack, store lumber flat, and weigh it down at each end and in the center to prevent warping and other distortions. Weighting is most important if the wood has a high moisture content.

Carrying materials
Pick up sheet goods by lifting from the knees. Balance the sheet against your shoulder. Plywood carriers, a hook with a long handle, are available so you don't have to lift the sheet so high. Carry long boards on your shoulder.

1×3

1×4

Keep materials off floor; add height if moisture is likely.

Selecting nails

Many types and sizes of nails are available, each one engineered for a specific use. The differences may seem small, but they can have a significant effect on the soundness and appearance of your job. Here's a guide to choosing among the standard types of nails:

Use **common** nails and **box** nails for framing jobs. Box nails are a bit thinner, for lighter work. **Cement-coated** nails drive more easily and hold more firmly. Attach drywall to framing with **drywall** nails. Use **roofing** nails for roof shingles and wherever a wide head is needed to hold material that might tear if a smaller head is used. Choose hot-dipped over electroplated galvanized nails; they last much longer.

Casing and **finishing** nails handle medium- and heavy-duty finishing work. For very fine work use **wire brads**. **Ringshank** and **spiral** nails grab wood tighter than conventional nails. Specially hardened **masonry** nails penetrate mortar joints, brick, and even concrete. **Corrugated fasteners** are used mainly for strengthening wood joints; they do not hold well by themselves.

Nails are normally sold in various-size boxes. If you are planning a large project, buying a large box usually saves you some money.

Types of nails

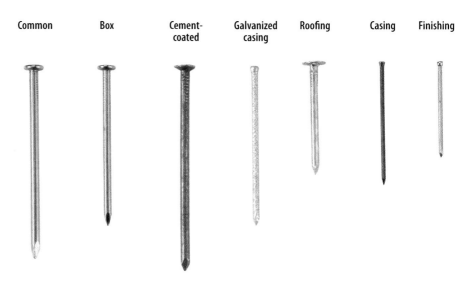

Common   Box   Cement-coated   Galvanized casing   Roofing   Casing   Finishing

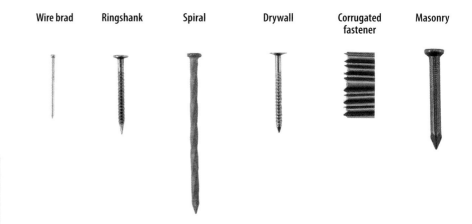

Wire brad   Ringshank   Spiral   Drywall   Corrugated fastener   Masonry

PENNIES AND INCHES

In Britain in the 1400s, so one story goes, 100 medium-size nails cost eight pennies. It didn't take long for the price to creep up, but we still use the term "penny" to express nail sizes. The abbreviation "d" for penny comes from *denarius,* a small, silver Roman coin used in Britain that equated with a penny.

Inch equivalent of nail penny sizes:

3d=1¼"	10d=3"
4d=1½"	12d=3¼"
6d=2"	16d=3½"
7d=2¼"	20d=4"
8d=2½"	40d=5"

THE NAIL FOR THE JOB

Use nails three times as long as the thickness of the material you are fastening. For instance, to attach a 1×4 (¾ inch thick) to a 2×4, a 6d nail (2 inches long) is a bit short. An 8d nail (2½ inches long, a little more than three times the thickness of the 1×4) does better. Make sure the nail does not poke through the material to which you are fastening.

THE TIP OF A NAIL

The tip of a common, box, or finishing nail is not symmetrical. Viewed point on, the tip is diamond shaped, not square, due to the way these nails are stamped. If you start the nail so the flatter side of the diamond is parallel to the grain of the board you are nailing it into, you're less likely to split the wood than if the flat side were against the grain.

Selecting screws and bolts

For the few seconds they take to drive, nails do a remarkable holding job. Yet for the little extra time it takes to drive a screw, you get a tighter-holding fastener, a neater appearance, and another plus—ease of disassembly. In fact, drywall screws teamed with cordless electric drill/drivers have created a revolution in fasteners, leading to a range of screws ranging from **deck screws** to general-purpose **wood screws.**

The most common configurations for screws are the **slotted head** and the **phillips head**, which has an X-shaped slot. Square-drive screws are less common but are growing in popularity.

There are three head shapes from which to choose. A **flathead screw** can be driven flush with or slightly below the surface of the wood. Use **ovalhead screws** with **trim washers** for a finished appearance. Install **roundhead screws** when you want the screw head to show.

General-purpose or **drywall screws** offer an inexpensive and easy way to fasten items together. You can buy them by the pound, and they drive easily using a drill with a screwdriver bit. **Trim-head screws** use a smaller phillips or square-drive bit. They hold better than finishing nails but the countersunk hole is larger.

Use **masonry screws** (often referred to by the brand name Tap-Con) to fasten material to masonry or concrete surfaces. Simply drill the correct-size hole in the masonry surface and drive the screw. Drive a **hanger screw** into a ceiling joist and fasten the object to be hung using the nut and thread on the screw's lower half.

Use **lag screws** for heavy-duty fastening. Drill a pilot hole and drive the screw with a wrench. Thin metal can be joined with self-tapping **sheet-metal screws.**

Screws should be three times as long as the thickness of the material being fastened. When buying screws, specify the gauge (diameter) you want. The thicker the gauge, the greater its holding power. Make sure you have the correct-size drill bit if drilling pilot holes. (See the box below.) For more on driving screws, see pages 37–38.

A **machine bolt** has a head that can be turned with a wrench. **Carriage bolts** have round heads for a finished appearance. When buying bolts, be sure to get the correct diameter and length; the bolt must be longer than the materials you are fastening so you can add the nut and **washers.** (For more on fastening with bolts, see page 39.)

Types of screws, bolts, and accessories

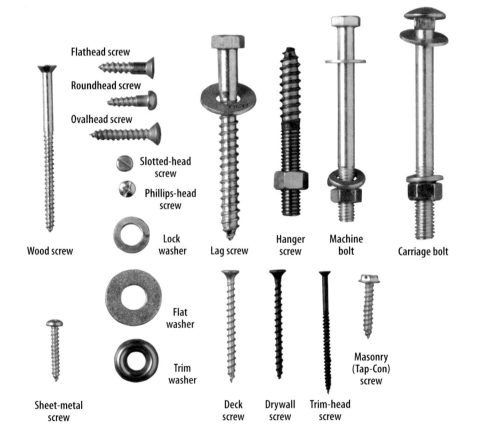

Flathead screw

Roundhead screw

Ovalhead screw

Slotted-head screw

Phillips-head screw

Lock washer

Wood screw

Lag screw

Hanger screw

Machine bolt

Carriage bolt

Flat washer

Trim washer

Sheet-metal screw

Deck screw

Drywall screw

Trim-head screw

Masonry (Tap-Con) screw

DRILLING PILOT HOLES

Prevent splitting the wood and make assembly easier by drilling pilot holes for screws. You also should drill pilot holes for nails near the end of a board, in thin material, or in hardwoods.

Standard wood screws require two holes: a shank hole to clear the unthreaded portion and a pilot hole for the threads. Drywall screws and similar kinds need only one hole size.

A chart of pilot-hole sizes for various screws is on page 98.

ADHESIVES

Adding glue strengthens any joint assembled with nails or screws. In some cases, such as edge-joining narrow boards to make a wider panel, glue is used without nails or screws. Such joints always should be clamped in accordance with the glue manufacturer's instructions. Glue characteristics are shown on page 98.

Selecting hardware

The items shown on these two pages represent just a sample of the options available in specialized hardware. At your hardware store or home center, you'll find a product designed for almost every conceivable carpentry need.

When you want to strengthen a wood joint, add a metal plate or brace, as shown at right. **Mending plates** reinforce end-to-end joints; **T-plates** handle end-to-edge joints. Flat corner irons strengthen corner joints by attaching to the face of the material; **angle brackets** do the same thing but attach to the inside or outside edges.

Shelf standards, as shown below right, come in a variety of configurations and finishes suitable for utilitarian or more decorative purposes. Most standards can be installed on the wall or into supports behind the shelves. Some standards can be installed on either side of shelves. **Adjustable standards and brackets** come in a variety of colors, sizes, and finishes. Use **utility brackets** for nonadjustable shelving in places where appearance is not important. **Closet rod brackets** let you attach a shelf and a closet rod to the same piece of hardware.

A large choice of door and cabinet hardware is available, as shown on the opposite page. Most full-size doors hang on the classic **butt hinge** (see page 124). For extra household security, add a **chain lock** to your door. **Piano hinges** mount flush on cabinets and chests, combining great strength with a slim, finished look. **Strap hinges** and **T-hinges** often are used on gates and trunk lids.

Cabinet hinges are available in four basic types. Decorative hinges work only for doors that are flush with the frame. Use **front-** or **side-mount offset hinges** for doors that are flush with the frame or have lips that overlap the frame. If a door completely overlies the frame, use a **pivot hinge** or a self-closing **European-style hidden hinge**. To open your cabinet doors, fit them with **knobs** or **pulls,** available in myriad sizes and styles. **Friction, roller, bullet,** or **magnetic catches** keep cabinet doors closed. (If you are using self-closing hinges, catches aren't necessary.)

For smooth-operating drawers, choose side-mounted **drawer slides** like the one shown on the next page.

Select appropriate joint reinforcement

For a quick and fairly permanent joint or repair, use inexpensive plates like these. Clamp the material together before attaching the plates. Drill pilot holes as centered as possible; otherwise, screws may pull the joint apart as they are driven.

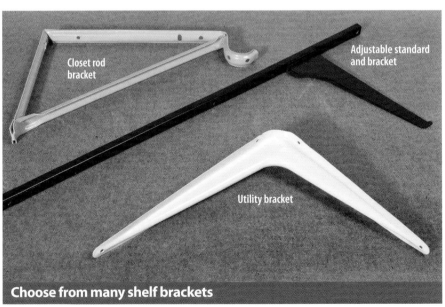

Choose from many shelf brackets

If you've ever tried to make a shelf bracket out of lumber, you'll realize how much time and effort is saved by using these handy pieces of hardware. For more on installing shelf hardware and shelf construction, see pages 102–103.

Door, gate, and bench hardware

Cabinet hardware

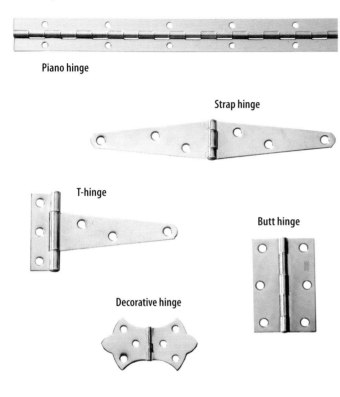

Piano hinge

Strap hinge

T-hinge

Butt hinge

Decorative hinge

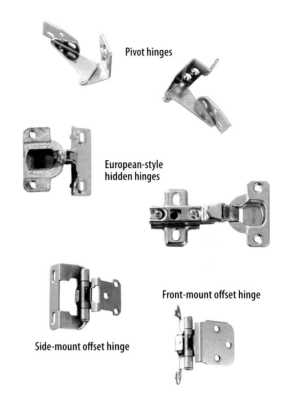

Pivot hinges

European-style
hidden hinges

Front-mount offset hinge

Side-mount offset hinge

Latch, lock, and handle hardware

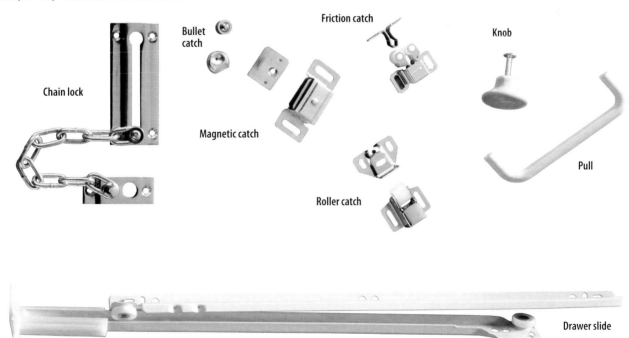

Chain lock

Bullet
catch

Friction catch

Knob

Magnetic catch

Roller catch

Pull

Drawer slide

Glue and fastener reference

You'll find many kinds of glue at a home center or hardware store, but not all are suited to all uses. The chart at bottom identifies some that are useful for carpentry and woodworking. Refer to the charts below and right for pilot-hole sizes for various kinds of screws.

HOLE SIZES, STANDARD WOOD SCREWS

Screw gauge	Shank hole	Pilot hole Hardwood	Softwood	Head counterbore
2	$3/32"$	$1/16"$	$1/16"$	$11/64"$
3	$7/64"$	$1/16"$	$1/16"$	$13/64"$
4	$7/64"$	$5/64"$	$1/16"$	$15/64"$
5	$1/8"$	$5/64"$	$1/16"$	$1/4"$
6	$9/64"$	$3/32"$	$5/64"$	$9/32"$
7	$5/32"$	$7/64"$	$3/32"$	$5/16"$
8	$5/32"$	$7/64"$	$3/32"$	$11/32"$
9	$11/64"$	$1/8"$	$7/64"$	$23/64"$
10	$3/16"$	$1/8"$	$7/64"$	$25/64"$
12	$7/32"$	$9/64"$	$1/8"$	$7/16"$
14	$1/4"$	$5/32"$	$9/64"$	$1/2"$

HOLE SIZES, DRYWALL/DECK SCREWS

(Drill one hole size through both parts to be joined.)

Screw gauge	Pilot hole Hardwood	Softwood	Head counterbore
4	$5/64"$	$1/16"$	$7/32"$
6	$7/64"$	$3/32"$	$17/64"$
8	$1/8"$	$7/64"$	$11/32"$
10	$9/64"$	$1/8"$	$23/64"$
12	$5/32"$	$9/64"$	$7/16"$
14	$3/16"$	$5/32"$	$1/2"$

GLUES FOR CARPENTRY

Type	Common name/brands	Comments
PVA (polyvinyl acetate)	White glue: Elmer's glue	Strong, not waterproof, long open (working) time, not gap-filling; joints must fit well; corrodes metal; not for gluing hardware to wood.
Aliphatic resin	Yellow glue: Elmer's carpenter's glue, Titebond	Stronger than white glue; moisture-resistant but not waterproof; grabs fast; shorter open time than white glue; not for gluing metal to wood; the most common woodworking glue.
Modified PVA	Titebond II, Elmer's Weather-Tite wood glue	Waterproof; stands weather exposure but not submersion, as in marine use; other characteristics similar to yellow glue; often used for general woodworking.
Liquid hide glue	Franklin hide glue	An easier-to-use version of the traditional hot hide glue, but used at room temperature straight from the bottle; mainly for wood-to-wood joints; long setting time; strong; heat and moisture weaken bond.
Polyurethane	Gorilla glue	Expands in joint; develops high strength; cures quickly; moisture speeds curing time; waterproof for weather exposure.
Cyanoacrylate ester	Instant glue, superglue, CA.	Strong, but not shock-resistant; bonds instantly, so doesn't require clamps; little or no gap-filling capability; requires care in use—bonds to skin instantly; glues many materials to each other.
Epoxy	Five-minute epoxy, two-ton epoxy	Another glue good for a variety of materials; comes in five-minute-setting and longer-setting varieties; two components, mix 1:1 before application; strong; water-resistant.
Construction adhesive	Liquid Nails, panel adhesive, Pliobond	Usually sold in caulking tubes; thick, strong, with several formulations available for a variety of purposes; for rough carpentry and framing, drywall, paneling, flooring, and other general use.

CARPENTRY
PROJECTS

Building a workbench

- **TIME:** About 4 hours
- **SKILLS:** Precise measuring and cutting, gluing, nailing, driving screws
- **TOOLS:** Tape measure, circular saw or tablesaw, drill and driver bit, hammer, nail set

Strength and durability define a well-built workbench. The heavy-duty legs of this workbench provide the strength to support large projects. The double-layered top withstands the blows of pounding. You can build the bench so the top layer can be removed and replaced with a new hardboard surface when it becomes damaged.

Load up the bottom shelf with tools and materials—the extra weight makes the bench more stable. The perforated hardboard back provides handy tool storage. If you want to skip the tool board, just cut the back legs to the same length as the front ones.

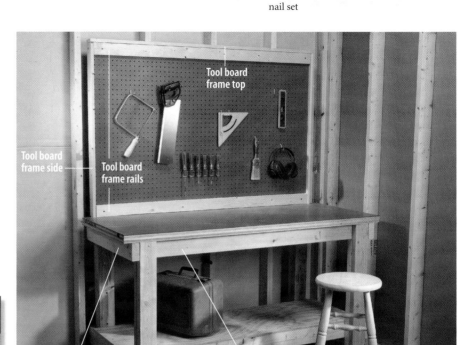

Tool board frame top

Tool board frame side

Tool board frame rails

Side braces

Rails

PARTS

Quantity	Piece	Length
2	2×4 rear legs	$69^5/_8$"
2	2×4 front legs	32"
4	2×4 short legs	$28^1/_2$"
4	2×4 rails	54"
4	2×4 side braces	$25^3/_8$"
1	$^1/_2$" plywood shelf	$19^3/_8$"×57"
2	$^3/_4$" plywood top	$23^7/_8$"×60"
1	$^1/_8$" tempered hardboard	$23^7/_8$"×60"
1	$^1/_4$" perforated hardboard	36"×54"
2	1×3 tool board frame sides	36"
1	1×3 tool board frame top	$55^1/_2$"
2	1×3 tool board frame rails	54"

Short leg

Front leg

1 Assemble the legs

Attach the short legs to the front and rear legs using glue and $2^1/_2$-inch drywall screws. The short legs are flush at one end with each front and rear leg. Use a drill with the proper-size phillips-head driver bit to make short work of the assembly.

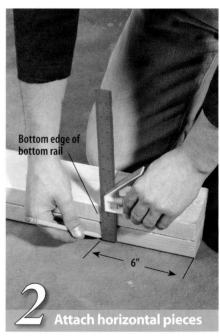

Bottom edge of bottom rail

6"

2 Attach horizontal pieces

Lay out lines 6 inches from the bottom of the legs to locate the bottoms of the lower rails and the side braces. Screw the bottom rails to the inside of the legs and the top rails into the leg notches, flush to the outside of the legs. Then screw the side braces to the outside of the legs, flush to the outside of the legs.

Rail

Rail

Side brace

Front leg — Short leg

Rail

Side brace

3 Attach the lower shelf

Place the lower shelf on top of the lower rails and side braces. Secure it with 1¼-inch drywall screws.

4 Construct the top

Put the first layer of plywood in place against the back leg extensions and centered side to side. Fasten it to the rails and side braces with 1¼-inch drywall screws. Screw the second plywood piece in place with 3-inch drywall screws driven through both layers of plywood into the bench.

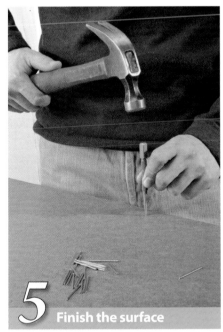

5 Finish the surface

Place the ⅛-inch hardboard on top of the plywood top, flush on all sides. Drive 4d finishing nails through the work surface into the plywood. Drive the nails slightly below the surface using a nail set. For a renewable surface, attach the hardboard with #6×¾-inch flathead screws.

6 Install the tool panel

Place the perforated hardboard against the tall back legs with its bottom edge resting on the bench surface. Attach the perforated hardboard to the leg extensions with ¾-inch drywall screws.

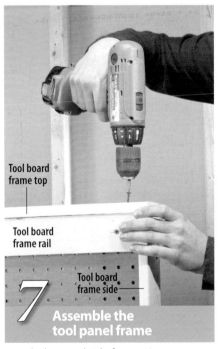

Tool board frame top

Tool board frame rail

Tool board frame side

7 Assemble the tool panel frame

Attach the panel side frame pieces to the tall back legs with ¾-inch drywall screws. Attach the rails to the legs with 2-inch drywall screws. Drive ¾-inch screws through the perforated hardboard into the backs of the rails. Use 1½-inch screws to attach the top board to the leg extensions and top rail.

Building shelves

■ **TIME:** 2 hours to make the project shown on this page

■ **SKILLS:** Precise measuring and cutting, fastening

■ **TOOLS:** Circular saw, tablesaw, or radial arm saw, layout square, pencil, hammer, chisel, strap clamp

You can build this simple dadoed shelf unit easily, altering the dimensions (see illustration on opposite page) to fit your needs. Though the project is relatively simple, you must measure and cut carefully. The mitered corners need to fit tightly for strength and appearance. Making straight cuts is difficult if the boards are warped or bowed, so choose the straightest boards you can find. The end result, a unit custom-made for your space, will be worth the effort.

To make the project even simpler, you can make butt joints between the top and bottom and the sides as shown in some of the illustrations on the opposite page.

1 Cut the sides, top, and bottom

Cut 45-degree bevels on both ends of the two sides, the top, and the bottom. Be sure the saw is set accurately to a 45-degree bevel; make test cuts on scrap wood. Use a tablesaw or a radial arm saw, or hold a layout square firmly against a factory edge as you cut with a circular saw. Measure from outside to outside—from the tip of one cut to the tip of the next.

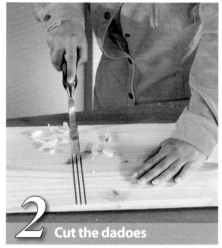

2 Cut the dadoes

Set the two vertical outside pieces side by side and mark them for the ¾-inch dadoes. Set the depth of your saw blade so it cuts ¼ inch deep. Make a series of cuts (see pages 47–48). Clean out the dadoes by cutting out remaining wood with a chisel, then smooth the bottom with the chisel held bevel side down.

3 Measure for the shelves

Temporarily fasten the box together by drilling pilot holes and partially driving (tacking) finishing nails at each corner. Or use a strap clamp (see page 43). Check the box for square. Measure from the inside of each dado to the inside of the corresponding dado to determine the length of each shelf. Cut the shelves to length.

4 Assemble the pieces

Disassemble the box. Apply glue and drive the nails that hold one side piece to the top and bottom pieces. Carefully position these fastened pieces so the side piece is lying on a flat surface. Dry-fit the shelves into the dadoes and set the remaining sidepiece in place. Disassemble and make any needed adjustments. Apply glue, check for square, and nail.

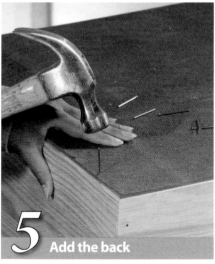

5 Add the back

Cut a piece of ¼-inch plywood or ⅛-inch hardboard for the back. The material should be ¼ inch smaller than the outside dimensions of the unit, so the backing edge is ⅛ inch inside the outer edge. Use the back to check that the unit is square. Leaving a ⅛-inch gap on all edges, fasten with 4d box nails every 4 inches. Fasten the back to the inner shelves as well.

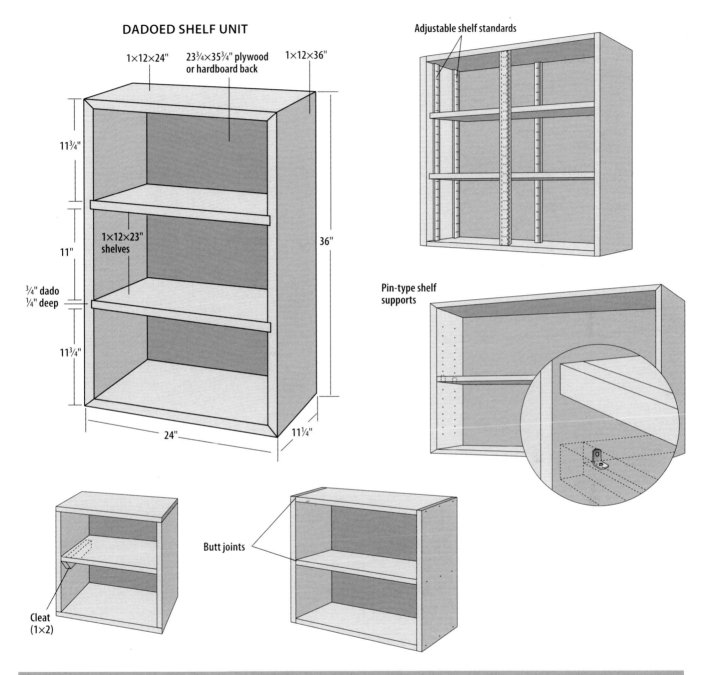

DADOED SHELF UNIT

1×12×24"
23¾×35¾" plywood or hardboard back
1×12×36"

11¾"

1×12×23" shelves

11"

¾" dado
¼" deep

11¾"

36"

24"
11¼"

Adjustable shelf standards

Pin-type shelf supports

Cleat (1×2)

Butt joints

Choose adjustable or fixed shelving

When building a shelf system using adjustable standards and clips and a central vertical support, the adjustable shelves must be shorter than the top and bottom. For a cleaner look, set the metal standards into grooves. To make pin-type adjustable shelves, precisely lay out the locations of the holes on the sidepieces by clamping the sides together before marking. Use a sharp bit that will not chip the surface of the wood as you bore the holes (brad-point bits work well). If a pin-type adjustable shelf unit is taller than 4 to 5 feet, it should have one or more fixed shelves to keep the sidepieces from bowing out. You can add an angle bracket or wooden cleat to which you can attach the fixed shelf.

The simplest unit has shelves screwed into place without dadoes. Such a unit is quite strong, as long as you use three or

more screws at each joint and the screws are fastened firmly. Drill pilot holes to avoid splitting the wood. Countersink the screw heads and fill the holes with putty or plugs. (See pages 33–34.) If you use trim-head screws, the holes will not be much larger than those for finishing nails. To make such shelves even stronger, add cleats.

A cleat-supported shelf is simple to build and ideal for utility areas. Use 1×2s for the cleats. Cut the front edge of each cleat at a 45-degree angle so it's not as noticeable. Secure the cleat with countersunk screws.

Dadoed shelves are stronger and present a clean, finished look because there is no hardware to hide. (See opposite page for instructions to build this unit.)

Hanging shelves and cabinets

- **TIME:** About 2 hours to hang an average shelf or cabinet system
- **SKILLS:** Measuring, plumbing, leveling, driving screws, finding wall studs
- **TOOLS:** Tape measure, drill, screwdriver, level, stud finder, awl

Any shelf system, be it simple boards or a cabinet with doors, must hang securely on a wall. If it is not anchored into wall studs, it probably will come loose when weight is put onto it. If it is not plumb and level, it will look shoddy and may even prove unsafe. As you plan your shelving, decide the following:

Are the shelves supported at their ends (by the side of the shelf unit or cabinet) or from the back?

Do you want the shelves to be adjustable or fixed? Shelves in living areas require the versatility of adjustable hardware; utility shelves used for storage in closets, garages, and basements are fine with fixed supports.

Select the hardware that suits your purposes best. The chart at right shows the most common options.

To make sure the shelves won't sag over time, use the shelving spans chart to determine the correct distance between shelf supports. The spacings listed assume that shelves are fully loaded with books—most likely the heaviest load they have to bear.

If you opt for fixed shelves, measure the tallest items slated to go onto the shelves and add at least 1 inch for overhead clearance.

PLANNING YOUR SHELF LAYOUT

- It may seem time-consuming, but you'll end up saving time by drawing a detailed plan of your shelf or cabinet system. Without a plan, it's hard to buy materials and easy to overlook hard-to-correct design flaws.
- Make sure unsupported shelf ends extend no more than one-third the distance allowed between the shelf standards.
- If you build a unit with fixed shelves, maximize space by tailoring the vertical spacing so your possessions fit exactly. Your storage and shelving needs may change over time, so adjustable shelves offer the most flexibility.

SHELF HARDWARE OPTIONS

Item	Application
	Rigid pressed-steel angle brackets hold medium-weight loads. For heavier loads, choose brackets reinforced with triangular gussets. Mount the longer leg against the wall and be sure upper screws are fastened firmly.
	When you can mount only on a wall or in the back of a cabinet, brackets that clip into slotted standards are the best way to provide adjustable support. Choose 8-, 10-, or 12-inch brackets.
	For adjustable shelves with a finished appearance, mount shelves onto the ends by popping pin-type clips into predrilled holes. The clips are relatively inexpensive, but the holes must be drilled precisely.
	These end-mounted adjustable standards and clips are strong but less attractive than other alternatives. For a dressier look, set the standards into grooves cut into the cabinet sides.
	Light-duty wire brackets are among the many accessories you can mount on perforated hardboard. Measure the thickness of the board before you buy it; $\frac{1}{4}$- and $\frac{1}{8}$-inch perforated hardboard require different bracket types.

SHELVING SPANS

Material used	Maximum span	Material used	Maximum span
$\frac{3}{4}$-inch plywood	32"	2×6, 2×8 lumber	36"
$\frac{3}{4}$-inch particleboard	24"	2×10, 2×12 lumber	48"
1×6, 1×8 lumber	18"	$\frac{1}{2}$-inch acrylic sheet	18"
1×10, 1×12 lumber	24"	$\frac{3}{8}$-inch glass	16"

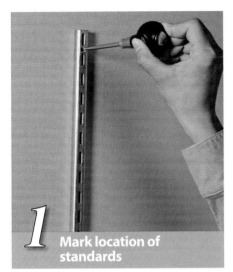

1 Mark location of standards

Find at least two wall studs to support the shelf standards. To find a stud, tap the wall until you hear a dull, not a hollow, sound or use a stud finder. Hammer in a small finishing nail to confirm you've found the stud. Hold one standard at the desired location and height. Mark for the top hole with an awl, then drill a pilot hole.

2 Plumb and secure the standard

Drive in and partially tighten the screw at the top of the standard. Using a carpenter's level, plumb the dangling standard, then use an awl to mark for the bottom hole. Attach the standard, check again that it is plumb, and finish securing it.

3 Mark for the other standards

Run a straightedge and level from the top of the standard to the approximate location of the last standard. Strike an erasable line and step back to see if the line looks level. If it doesn't, redraw the line so it's parallel to the floor or ceiling. Install the first and last standards, making sure their top ends are up.

4 Install intermediate standards

If shelves are to bear heavy loads, install intermediate standards to prevent sagging. Mark the position between the end standards. Place a shelf bracket at the same location on both end standards and locate the intermediates by laying a straightedge across the brackets.

Mount a cabinet or shelf unit

Of the many ways to hang cabinets on walls, the one shown above is one of the best. It provides plenty of holding power without visible screw heads or supports. It's also easy to level; you need only level the back cleat. The back of the unit, however, must be recessed 3/4 inch.

Cut a 1×4 to fit behind the cabinet. Make a beveled rip cut along its centerline (see pages 27–28). Attach one of the pieces to the cabinet. Level and secure the other to the wall. Lift the unit and hold it against the wall, then slide it down onto the piece attached to the wall.

If a cabinet is well-constructed, another approach is to attach it to the wall simply by holding it in place and driving screws through the cabinet back into wall studs. Place screws where they will be least visible.

Building decorative molding shelves

■ **TIME:** About 2 hours to build a set of three shelves
■ **SKILLS:** Measuring, marking, cutting miters into crown molding
■ **TOOLS:** Miter box and backsaw or power mitersaw, hammer, nail set, clamps

Make the most of wall space with a decorative shelf constructed with trim molding. Set it alone to draw the eye or cover a wall to create an architectural statement. Make the shelf deep enough to hold a gallery of framed photographs of family, friends, and cherished pets and small objects. Adjust the depth of the top shelf to 10 inches and go for an eclectic effect by displaying candles, objets d'art, or flowers.

Display collectibles

Decorative shelves lend an architectural line to any room while creating a focal point for art and collectibles.

Suit a modern style

Decorative shelves can enhance the look of a modern decorating scheme with minimal effort. Instead of combining various molding to create the molding shelves, cut single pieces of wood to the length of your shelf as shown at right.

1 **Cut the shelf**

Use a miter box and backsaw or power mitersaw to cut the length of the top of your shelf. Good lengths for a shelf are 2, 3, or 4 feet. A set of three shelves in varied lengths makes a nice grouping.

2 Cut the molding

Cut the molding ends with opposing 45-degree angles. Measure and cut the endpieces to abut the front molding. The sides of the endpieces that fit against the wall should be cut at 90 degrees to seat flush against the wall.

3 Apply glue

Apply wood glue to the surface areas of the molding and the shelf. Attach the front length of the crown molding to the shelf with glue (see pages 42–43).

4 Clamp together

Drive finishing nails through the crown molding into the top of the shelf. Apply glue to the endpieces and attach flush to the front molding with finishing nails. Set the nails using a nail set.

5 Fill nail holes

Fill the nail holes with a wood filler and allow to dry. If shrinkage occurs, apply more wood filler (see pages 57–58).

6 Sand smooth

Sand to finish. Start with a coarse-grit sandpaper. Gradually work to a fine-grit sandpaper for a smooth finish (see pages 55–56).

7 Finish with paint

Apply primer for painting or stain and apply a clear-coat sealant. To install the shelf, locate wall studs with a stud finder. Attach a cleat to the wall and fit the shelf over the cleat. Secure with countersunk screws down through the shelf into the cleat.

Organizing a bedroom closet

■ **TIME:** For a typical 6-foot closet, one day to build an organizer

■ **SKILLS:** Measuring and cutting, fastening with screws or nails

■ **TOOLS:** Circular saw, tape measure, framing square, stud finder, chalkline, hammer, nail set, drill and screwdriver bit

A typical closet with a single hanging pole and one or two long shelves wastes a lot of space and is difficult to use. If you outfit your closet with custom-made organizers, your clothing fits without wasted space and you can easily get at the things you frequently need.

You can buy ready-made storage or shelf units that are easy to install, build your own shelves and dividers out of lumber, or use a combination of the two. Keep in mind that painting wood shelves often is more time-consuming than building them.

Precut material

It often is easier to precut materials and have them ready for installation. This requires careful planning and accurate measurements. Draw your new closet organizer to scale on graph paper. For this project materials were precut.

PLAN A WELL-ORGANIZED CLOSET

Measure and catalog your clothes and storage items. (See the chart below for some standard sizes.) By grouping clothes according to height, you can gain usable space. Measure the horizontal space needed for each type of clothing. Make a sketch of your ideal finished closet, taking into account the ¾-inch thickness of the boards.

Sometimes it makes sense to begin with a set of store-bought drawers and build shelves around it. Be sure the closet pole is well-supported every 4 feet, or in time it will sag.

Decide which storage items can be placed up high. Avoid tall stacks of clothes and use storage boxes or wire bins where possible.

Group for efficiency and organization

Once you've installed the custom-built closet organizer system, group clothes according to length, type, season, and color. By grouping similar types of clothing, you can quickly find what you want.

1 Attach the shelf supports

Measure and mark the locations of the top and bottom shelf supports on the back wall and sidewalls of the closet. A good height for the top shelf is 84 inches above the floor; for the bottom shelf, 76 inches. This provides plenty of storage room between the two shelves without making the top shelf unreachable. Mark the locations on the walls with a chalkline. Determine the locations of the wall studs using a stud finder and mark them. Studs provide support. Drive 8d finishing nails through the supports into the wall studs.

CLOTHING MEASUREMENTS

Women's Item	Length	Men's Item	Length	Accessory	Length
Long dress	69"	Topcoat	50"	Garment bag	57"
Robe	52"	Trousers (cuff-hung)	44"	Hanging shoe bag	36"
Coat	52"	Travel bag	41"	Umbrella or cane	36"
Dress	45"	Suit	38"		
Skirt	29"	Shirt	28"		
Suit	29"	Tie	27"		
Blouse	28"	Trousers (double-hung)	20"		

2 Assemble the center shelf unit

Space the center shelves evenly or according to your design plan. You may want to vary the shelf heights depending on the items you are storing. Drive 6d finishing nails to hold the shelves in place. Be sure to leave the top and bottom units open.

3 Position the center shelf unit

Position the center shelf unit where it best fits your needs. You could put it in the middle or offset it to provide more storage room on one side of the closet. Mark the location. Make sure that the top of the shelf unit is flush with the top of the lower shelf support bracket. If it is not, mark to cut so it is flush. Mark the top for a notch to fit over the lower shelf support. Remove the shelf and cut the notch with a circular saw or jigsaw. Align the center shelf unit with the mark. Check for level. Have a helper hold it in place while you set the lower shelf on the lower shelf support.

4 Set the top shelf

Drive 6d finishing nails through the lower shelf into the center of the shelf unit to hold it in place. Once attached, set the top shelf.

5 Install pole brackets

Measure for the locations of pole brackets on the shelf unit and mark. Install pole brackets, on whichever side of the center shelf you desire, at a height of 38 inches above the floor for a lower clothes pole. Attach a pole bracket to a stud at the opposite endwall of the closet, 3 inches from the bottom of the lower shelf. Attach pole brackets to the center shelf unit with screws.

Molding ideas

Dress up a room without using paint or wallpaper. Change just one subtle detail and make a statement. Trim adds a distinctive touch. Base molding frames walls. Crown molding adds elegance; it provides an architectural detail that gives character to a room. Trim molding can be a simple strip of wood or an elaborate creation incorporating different elements of designs, materials, and finishes. The following six pages show the basics of how to install base trim and crown molding.

Add visual interest to walls

Moldings help add drama to a room. In this living room, the walls are painted one rich hue and a band at the top of the wall between moldings a darker color. Moldings and trimwork in the room are painted white to add another accent.

Avoid cutting corners

Lightweight materials such as urethane foam make installing ornate moldings a snap. Crown moldings are available with preformed corner blocks and snap-on installation clips that eliminate the effort of precisely mitering the corners and nailing up moldings. You can combine pieces to create a custom look.

Installing base molding

■ **TIME:** About 10 minutes per piece of molding

■ **SKILLS:** Precise measuring and cutting, figuring out the direction of cuts, nailing

■ **TOOLS:** Tape measure, combination square, miter box and backsaw or power mitersaw, coping saw, rasp, block plane, hammer, nail set

Base molding runs along the bottom of the wall at the floor. Base moldings vary from simple square-edge boards to profiled moldings. Baseboards often are finished with a base shoe, a molding much like a quarter round that fits at the bottom of the base molding against the floor. When the wall is longer than available moldings, join two pieces with a butt splice in an inconspicuous location. Where the joint shows, use a scarf joint for a more professional look.

Installing molding to finish off a project can be the most gratifying part of the job. Although it's easier than you might expect, it takes some practice. Start installing molding where it is the least visible. You'll soon surprise yourself with your speed and neat joinery. The most common mistake is to cut a miter in the wrong direction. Whenever possible, mark pieces clearly, not only for length but also for the direction of the cut.

Base molding basics

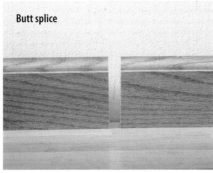

Butt splice

Install the corner piece first, then the baseboards.

45° scarf joint splice for a more finished look

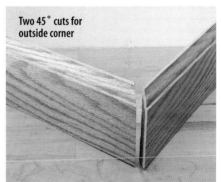

Two 45° cuts for outside corner

BUYING MOLDING

Molding can be expensive, so determine exactly how many pieces of each size you need. On a piece of paper make columns for each size—8 feet, 10 feet, 12 feet, etc. As you measure for individual pieces, tally how many you need under each column. If you have an old house, you may need moldings that are no longer made. A millwork company can probably make replicas. If the price is too high or you need only a small piece of molding, you may be able to make a reasonable facsimile using a router, tablesaw, radial arm saw, and belt sander.

Measure and mark precisely

Whenever possible, hold a piece of molding in place and mark it with a knife or sharp pencil rather than taking measurements with a tape.

1 **Start on a short wall**

If you have a piece of molding that is longer than the wall, you can install the base with just one strip. Cut each end at 90 degrees to run directly into each corner. Measure for the length of the next piece. If the wall is longer than the trim, you need to make a scarf joint splice. Try to place the cut so that it is over a stud.

Install door and window casing and other vertical molding before you install molding at the bottom of your walls. Choose from ranch or colonial base molding or use a three-piece base for a traditional look. It is best to add a quarter round or base shoe as well. These types bend easily with variations in the flooring and buffer molding from vacuum cleaner scuffs.

You may be tempted simply to miter-cut pieces for inside corners. This often leads to unsightly gaps and misaligned joints because the corners are almost never true 90-degree angles. Instead cut the first piece to length with a 90-degree cut and cope-cut the second piece to fit against it (see page 115).

Stain first but paint second: Stain molding before you install it. If you want to paint it, install the molding first, then paint.

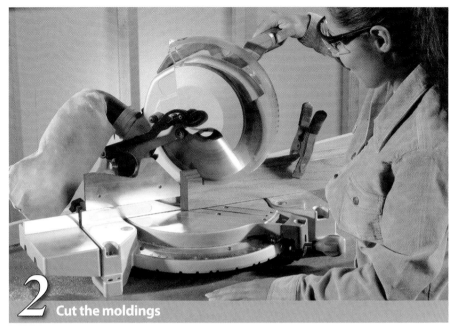

2 Cut the moldings

Sight down the blade of the saw and slide the molding until the saw cuts just to the scrap side of your mark. Grasp the molding tightly so it doesn't slide as you cut it. For a coped joint, cut the end at a 45-degree angle and highlight the profile with your pencil to make it easier to follow with your coping saw. Cut along the profile to make a back bevel cut. Finish

taking off the remaining back bevel with a half-round rasp until the piece sits squarely against your first piece with no gap.

For a scarf joint, cut the first molding's end at 45 degrees. Cut at a 45-degree angle on the next piece to mate with the first. Test-fit the joint.

3 Predrill

Predrill through both sides of a scarf joint. Prevent splitting by driving the nails ½ inch from the top and bottom of the molding. Slightly offset the nails at each stud location.

4 Glue the joint

Apply glue to connecting ends to strengthen the joint. Drive finishing nails to hold.

5 Work around the room

Continue to measure, cut, and install base molding around the room. When you get to an outside corner, set the first piece a bit long on the wall and mark it by setting your combination square at the corner. Mark the second piece the same way. Miter the ends and check that they meet neatly. If the joint is open at either the top or the bottom, trim each piece with a block plane or resaw it with a playing card between the piece and the saw fence to slightly change the angle. Install the moldings and set the nails below the surface.

6 Fill holes

Fill nail holes with wood filler. For stained or clear-finished baseboards, use filler that matches the wood. White filler is fine on painted woodwork. Some fillers shrink as they dry; you may need to wait and apply a second coat of filler.

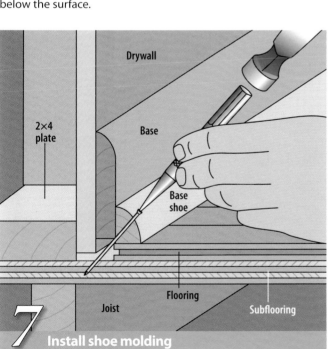

7 Install shoe molding

Predrill the shoe molding. Drive nails in so they miss the flooring, allowing it to move with changes in humidity without changing the position of the shoe molding.

ACHIEVE THAT PROFESSIONAL LOOK

Avoid splits. Thin stock and moldings are prone to splitting and cracking. Don't take chances. Wherever you are driving a nail within 3 inches of the edge of a piece, drill a pilot hole. You also can lightly blunt the tip of the nail by hitting it with a hammer. The blunted point cuts and tears through the wood fibers instead of wedging between them and splitting the wood.

The most common mistake when installing molding is using too many nails. Drive in only as many as you need to firmly hold the piece flush against the wall.

Installing crown molding

■ **TIME:** About 4 hours to install crown molding in a 12×12-foot room
■ **SKILLS:** Measuring precisely, cutting molding with miter box or mitersaw, coping cuts, nailing
■ **TOOLS:** Tape measure, miter box with backsaw or power mitersaw, coping saw, utility knife, hammer, nail set

The elegance and beauty of crown molding can transform a boxy room. With more and more molding profiles available, you have plenty of options for adding an attractive finishing touch to your home.

Although installing crown molding takes patience and a few tricks of the trade, homeowners who are comfortable with basic carpentry tools and who have coped molding joints should have few problems. Careful fitting and refitting are crucial to obtaining a close fit between sections of molding.

When buying trim, look for straight, solid pieces. Avoid warped or twisted pieces. Measure your wall lengths before purchasing trim. Whenever possible, purchase long enough pieces to avoid cuts.

Select from softwood or hardwood species. Softwoods such as pine, fir, and spruce are affordable and easy to work with. Hardwoods such as oak and maple tend to be more expensive and harder to work with.

To color match, pick molding from the same bundle at one store. Molding comes in stain-grade and paint-grade. Paint-grade molding usually is shorter pieces finger-jointed together. Stain-grade comes in continuous long pieces.

Store materials in the room you plan to trim. Letting the wood adjust to the environment for a couple of days avoids shrinkage problems later. Consider selecting trim that is primed on both sides, or prime it yourself.

When working over your head, a solid platform makes all the difference. Crown molding requires careful fitting and nailing, which can be difficult to do from a stepladder. Make the job easier by finding a couple of planks and two sturdy sawhorses to make a platform to stand on while installing the molding. In addition, enlist a helper to hold the lengths of molding while you measure, position, and fasten them.

Before beginning this challenging project, review marking and measuring techniques (pages 10–12), how to use a miter box (page 20), and nailing techniques (pages 35–36).

CAUTION

Remember to think upside down as you make miter cuts. Double-check which edge of the crown molding goes up—the difference is subtle.

BE SHARP

The right tools—kept clean and sharp—help make a precise job, such as installing crown molding, easier. Here are some tips:

Drop off your saw for professional sharpening well before you begin the job. A sharpened saw provides better control and a cleaner cut, and is easier to use.

Buy new coping-saw blades. They break easily, so have half a dozen on hand.

Have plenty of clamps to hold the molding while you cut it. The less you rely on your own holding power, the easier and more accurately you can make the saw cuts.

1 Start with a square cut

To achieve a mitered look in corners that are seldom perfectly square, run the first piece of crown molding tightly into the corners. Cope the mating pieces in the shape of the profile of the molding so they butt neatly against the face of the first piece.

2 Make a miter cut

To cope the molding, start with a miter cut that highlights the molding profile. Use a deep miter box and a fine-tooth backsaw or a power mitersaw. Position the molding so it is upside down in the miter box. The face of the molding that goes against the ceiling should be on the bottom of the miter box. For inside corners, the bottom of the molding is the longest edge.

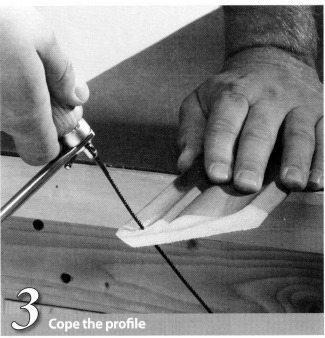

3 Cope the profile

If the mitered cut is correct, you should see the profile of the molding. Cut away the wood along the back side of the molding with a coping saw. Err on the side of removing too much rather than too little; only the outermost edge of the coped molding can be seen.

4 Fine-tune your cut

Use a utility knife or rasp to remove any excess material you missed with the coping saw. Be careful that you do not cut into the exposed face of the molding. Hold the piece in place to test the fit. Take the piece down and trim further if necessary.

5 Plan each joint

Map out the job so that one end of each piece of crown molding always is cut straight and one end is mitered and coped. Use butt joints for long runs. Save the most visible parts of the job for last, when you've honed your mitering, coping, and fitting skills.

6 Nail into place …

If the molding runs perpendicularly to the ceiling joists, determine the location of the joists. Drill pilot holes to keep the molding from splitting. As you attach the molding, tack it into place with a few nails. Take a good look at the positioning before completing the nailing.

Drywall nail — **Framing**

Drywall

Drywall screw

2×2 nailer —

6d finishing nail —

or add a nailer

To provide a solid nailing area where the joists run parallel to the crown molding, cut a beveled face onto a 2×2, as shown. Cut the 2×2 to length and screw it to the wall so it's in the corner formed by the ceiling and the wall. The 2×2 provides a surface, at the proper angle, to which you can nail the molding.

PRACTICE MAKES PERFECT

It is particularly important to gain some familiarity with the way molding is cut and coped. The more proficient you are at making overlapping joints, the less likely you are to make costly errors.

To avoid expensive mistakes with crown molding, hone your mitering and coping skills before you plunge into the job. Buy extra molding of the type you plan to use and cut a 2- or 3-foot piece for test cuts. Practice the steps shown on these pages.

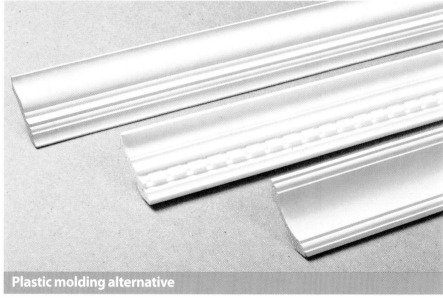

Plastic molding alternative

Synthetic materials have arrived as wood alternatives. The pieces don't shrink or warp the way some wood does, but can look wavy if not supported well. Manufacturers offer a variety of styles.

Plastic trim is lightweight and easy to cut and install. Some kinds install with clips, eliminating nailing. As with wood moldings, you can purchase corner blocks, eliminating miter cuts.

Wall frame ideas

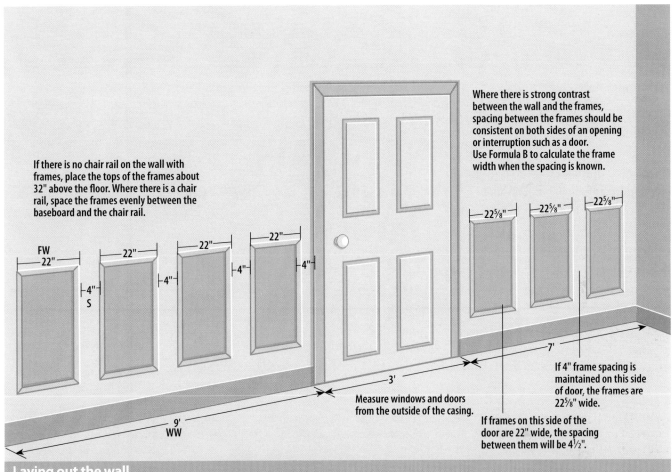

If there is no chair rail on the wall with frames, place the tops of the frames about 32" above the floor. Where there is a chair rail, space the frames evenly between the baseboard and the chair rail.

Where there is strong contrast between the wall and the frames, spacing between the frames should be consistent on both sides of an opening or interruption such as a door. Use Formula B to calculate the frame width when the spacing is known.

FW
22"

22"

22"

22"

4"
S

4"

4"

4"

22⅝"

22⅝"

22⅝"

9'
WW

3'

7'

Measure windows and doors from the outside of the casing.

If 4" frame spacing is maintained on this side of door, the frames are 22⅝" wide.

If frames on this side of the door are 22" wide, the spacing between them will be 4½".

Laying out the wall

Measure the wall and its doors and windows. Sketch the wall, then determine how many frames you want. A frame below a window should be the same width as the window. Estimate the length of each frame, then use Formula A in the box at the right to calculate the spacing. Adjust the frame length and spacing for the most pleasing effect.

On the wall shown, the spacing works out differently for the panels on each side of the door. You can vary either the frame width or the spacing to fit the frames onto the wall. In this case, it's probably better to keep the spacing consistent along the wall by changing the size of the three panels on the 7-foot wall, using Formula B at right. Adding ⅝" to each frame width is less noticeable than adding ½" to the 4" spaces between the frames.

FRAME SPACING

Formula A. This formula calculates the spacing between frames when the frame width is known. Decide how many frames are to fit on the wall, then calculate the space between the frames and at each end of the array (S) using the formula below. Express all measurements in the same unit.

$$S=\{WW-(FW\times F)\}\div(F+1)$$
WW=Width of wall
FW=Width of one frame
F=Number of frames

Example:
WW=9' (108"), FW=22", F=4
S={108"-88"}÷5
S=20"÷5
S=4"

Formula B. This formula calculates the frame width when spacing between the frames is known. Determine how many frames are to fit on the wall, then calculate the frame width (FW) using the formula below. Be sure to express all measurements in the same unit.

$$FW=\{WW-[S\times(F+1)]\}\div F$$
WW=Width of wall
S=Space between frames
F=Number of frames

Example:
WW=7'(84"), S=4", F=3
FW=84"-(4"×4)÷3
FW=68"÷3;
FW=22⅝" approximately

Installing wall frames

- **TIME:** About 1 day, longer if you need to address awkward situations
- **SKILLS:** Cutting, measuring, gluing, fastening with nails, sanding, painting, staining
- **TOOLS:** Tape measure, chalkline, pencil, framing square, saw, layout or combination square, level, power drill with screwdriver bit, scrap plywood, nail set, wood filler, hammer

Wall frames dress up any room. The three-dimensional frames divide the wall area into smaller geometric spaces. The design possibilities and combinations are unlimited. Wall frames create drama and add an element of interest.

Experiment with frame sizes and spacing. If you have space for only three frames in your design, make the middle frame wider. Create a rhythm by flanking a wide wall frame with narrower frames in a progression. The arrangement of proportional frames gives balance to a wall. With five frames you could make the middle and end frames narrower than the other two. See page 117 for more about spacing.

Keep an eye on scale. A well-designed room might include a base molding wider than a chair rail, a chair rail more massive than a door and window casing, and wall frames providing a delicate accent.

1 Make a template

Constructing a template makes easy work of building wall frames. Attach a piece of plywood cut to the inside dimensions of the frame to a larger piece of plywood. The plywood should be at least $\frac{1}{2}$ inch thick, allowing you to apply pressure for gluing mitered edges to create a tight joint. The bottom piece should extend $1\frac{1}{2}$ inches beyond the template to provide a base.

2 Glue the ends

Assemble the miter-cut pieces around the plywood template, gluing the mitered ends. Fasten with an air nailer or use a hammer with finishing nails. Prevent the frame ends from splitting by predrilling the holes. Drive the nailheads below the surface with a nail set.

3 Snap a chalkline

Measure from the bottom of the chair rail to the top of the wall frame (or from the top of the baseboard to the top of the frame) at opposite ends of the wall. Stretch a chalkline between the points and snap it for a guideline. See page 117 for more information on arranging frames on a wall.

4 Mark molding placement

Mark the top corners of each wall frame on the chalkline. Make two guides from scraps: one the interval width between frames and one the width to the chair rail.

5 Level the frame

Apply adhesive to the back of the frame and position it on the wall using the chalkline and your guides. Check for level.

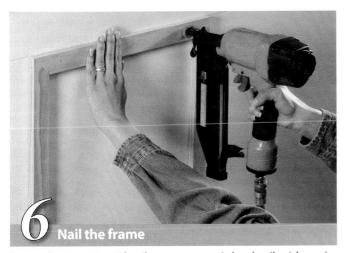

6 Nail the frame

Fasten the top using 6d nails or a pneumatic brad nailer (shown). Make sure the frame is plumb and level.

7 Secure the sides and bottom

Fasten the sides, then the bottom of the frame. Set the nails below the wood surface.

8 Apply wood filler

Fill the holes with wood filler. Caulk the gaps on the inside and outside. Allow to dry.

9 Finish the surface

Sand to finish (see pages 55–56). Prime and paint, or stain and seal.

Planning for a chair rail

Chair rail molding protects the wall from chairs, but this is only one of the uses of this versatile molding. Use it as casing, base, wallpaper border, or panel molding. A chair rail is a dramatic addition to any room.

A basic chair rail is a molding that runs around your room's perimeter about one-third of the way up the wall. Many people like to dress the walls above and below the chair rail. For example you may wish to paint the sections of the wall different colors or wallpaper one section and paint the other. You also may paint or stain the chair rail the same color as or a different color from the background wall.

Divide a wall for drama

A chair rail like this one suggests painting the wall in two colors. After you have completed the steps for installing a chair rail on page 121, consider the color scheme you want to use.

For a subtle look, choose two shades of the same color. For a more dramatic look, use a light and a dark color. Paint the darker shade below the chair rail to visually anchor the space.

Display art

Create a picture rail like this one by adding a wide top cap to crown molding placed at chair rail height. Pictures easily can be repositioned along the molding to accommodate a changing collection.

Installing a chair rail

■ **TIME:** 3 to 4 hours
■ **SKILLS:** Cutting, measuring, gluing, fastening with nails, sanding, painting, staining
■ **TOOLS:** Tape measure, chalkline, pencil, framing square, saw, layout or combination square, level, miter box or mitersaw, nail set, wood filler, hammer

Traditionally chair rails protected walls from chairs. Wallcoverings above the chair rail stayed clean while the painted area below the molding could be washed, repaired, or repainted to hide wear and tear. Today chair rails are more decorative.

A chair rail is usually positioned 32 inches above the floor—one-third the height of an 8-foot wall. The steps show how to build a custom chair rail by attaching stock chair rail molding and cove trim to a support board on the wall. The support piece should be the width of the chair rail and ½ inch thick. You can install a stock molding without the support piece and extra trim.

1 Snap a chalkline

Establish the height of the chair rail. Mark the height at a couple of locations along each wall. Stretch a chalkline along the marks. Check for level. Snap the chalkline to establish a guideline.

2 Level the wall trim

Align the support piece along the line. Have a helper hold the piece in place and level it. Attach the board to the wall with finishing nails or a pneumatic finishing nailer.

3 Measure the moldings

Measure the length of the wall trim and cut a piece of cove molding to length for the cap. Hold the chair rail in position against the door casing and mark the end for a 45-degree cut.

4 Glue the rail

Apply wood glue along the top of the support board. This provides additional strength for the cap.

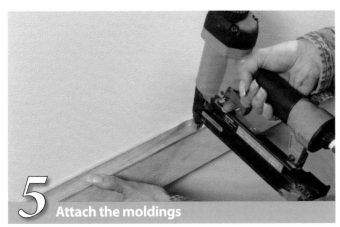

5 Attach the moldings

Fasten the cap rail to the support board. Butt the cap against the door casing. Attach the chair rail to the face of the support board. Install another cove molding on the bottom if you wish.

6 Sand the rail

Set all nails below the surface. Fill the holes with wood filler, let dry, and sand to finish. Prime and paint, or stain and seal.

Solving door problems

■ **TIME:** 1 to 2 hours to diagnose and repair a door

■ **SKILLS:** Close observation, planing, fastening screws

■ **TOOLS:** Screwdriver, hammer, nail set, plane, chisel

If a door sticks or does not close properly, don't assume that you need to remove it and plane it. Analyze the situation while the door is in place. Often screws holding the top hinge come loose, causing the door to lean. Remount the screws. (See far right.)

Loose screws, however, may be a symptom of other problems. Close the door, watching the hinge leaf that is connected to the jamb. If the hinge leaf moves, it is under stress and will come loose again. Check where the door is rubbing, scribe a line along it, and plane it.

WHERE'S THE RUB

When a door sticks, it is not always obvious just where the door is rubbing against the jamb. Close the door and insert a piece of cardboard into the gap between the door and the jamb. Slide it until you find a tight spot; that's where the door is sticking. For an exterior door, test the threshold as well.

Before scribing a mark to plane a sticking door (see page 16), close the door to the point where it begins to stick, and no farther. If the door is significantly too wide, remove the door and plane it until it closes without straining. Then complete the planing.

Use cardboard to shim a door

If your door is rubbing against the jamb on the hinge side, you can relieve the pressure by shimming the hinges out. Unscrew the part of the hinge connected to the jamb and insert a piece of cardboard behind it. If a door binds at the top of the strike jamb, you may be able to fix it by shimming out the bottom hinge.

Remount and tighten screws

If hinge screws are loose, wedge the door open and remove the screws. Fold back the hinge, taking care not to lose shims that may be behind it. Whittle hole-size pieces of wood or dowels, add carpenter's glue, and push the wood into the holes. Chisel the plugs flush, fold the hinge back, drill pilot holes, and drive the screws.

Remove a door

If your door needs to be modified so it fits, mark it with clear scribe lines. You probably need to remove the door to get at the edges that need planing. Tap the hinge pins out with a nail set, removing the bottom pin first. If the hinges are old and the pins are solidly rusted or painted in place, unscrew the hinges from the door to remove it.

Plane the door

To plane the edge, stand the door on its edge on a flat surface. Brace it in a corner so it will stay still as you work. If you need to plane the top or bottom of the door, work from each end toward the middle to avoid splintering at the edges (see pages 53–54). If you have to shorten a door, cut the door with a circular saw (opposite page), then plane it smooth.

Move the stop to correct a bind

Sometimes a door binds against the stop on the hinge side or it doesn't close completely because the stop on the latch side is placed improperly. In either case, it is easier to move the stop than to unwarp a door. Pry the stop off. Close the door and scribe a line on the jamb along the door's edge. Nail the stop on this line.

Shim a strike plate

If a strike plate is too far away for the door latch to engage it, shim it out with cardboard. Often a latch and strike get out of alignment because the house has settled. If this occurs, unscrew the strike, chisel out a new mortise, drill pilot holes, and reinstall the strike. Fill the old mortise cavity with wood putty and sand it smooth.

QUIETING SQUEAKS

Solving noisy door problems may be as simple as oiling the hinges. Before removing the door or the hinges, open the door and oil the hinges with lightweight oil. Then open and close the door several times.

If oiling does not solve the problem, prop open the door with shims at the floor and remove a hinge pin. Clean rust off the hinge pin and clean out the pinholes in the hinge, using a pipe cleaner or rolled-up emery cloth. Oil the parts and replace the hinge pin. Repeat this process for the other hinge(s). Do not tap the hinge pins all the way down; leave a little gap so they can be pried out easily. Still squeaking? Replace the hinges.

Cutting a door

- **TIME:** About 2 hours to cut down a hollow-core door
- **SKILLS:** Measuring, cutting a straight line, smoothing
- **TOOLS:** Knife, circular saw, straightedge, chisel, hammer

To avoid splintering the door face, score a line with a knife wherever you cut across the grain on a door. Then make your saw cut below that line with a smooth-cutting blade.

Solid-core doors are filled with particleboard; there is solid wood for only about an inch around the perimeter. If you cut more than an inch, the exposed particleboard requires a couple of coats of sealer.

Trimming a hollow-core door is more complex. (See steps, right.)

1 Cut the veneer, then the door

With a straightedge clamped in position, cut through the veneer with a sharp utility knife about $\frac{1}{16}$ inch above where you want your final cut. It may take several passes with your knife to do this. Move the straightedge into final position, clamp it, and complete the cut with a circular saw (see page 18).

2 Insert a filler

If you cut off more than 2 inches of a hollow-core door, the door will be hollow at the place you just cut. Clear out some of the cardboard webbing with a chisel. Rip and crosscut a piece of softwood to the required width and length. Apply carpenter's glue to both sides of the piece and tap the piece into position. Clamp firmly until the glue has set.

Installing door hinges

A door that swings easily on neatly installed hinges is the hallmark of a good carpenter. Hanging a door requires care and patience. If you work carefully and pay attention to details, you can install a door that swings freely and shuts firmly.

If you are replacing an old door, the door opening may not be square. Most homes settle over the years, causing door opening shapes to shift.

Cutting the door to fit the opening is the first and most difficult task. If the old door fits well, use it as a template. Simply remove the old hardware, lay the door on top of your new door, and trace around it for trimming. If the old door did not fit well, have a helper hold the new door in place while you shim it into final position. Carefully mark trimming points. If the doorjamb is damaged and must be replaced, take care to square the new jamb as you install it or install a prehung door (see page 127).

Hanging a door involves a strict order. First hang the door and make sure it swings freely and closes tightly against the door stop. Next install the lockset. Finally cut the hole for and install the strike plate.

- **TIME:** About 3 hours to hang a door and install a new lockset and deadbolt
- **SKILLS:** Measuring precisely, chiseling, drilling, fastening with screws
- **TOOLS:** Drill with the correct bits (check the lockset instructions), utility knife or butt marker, tape measure, center punch, screwdriver, hammer, chisel, awl

ROUTING MORTISES

A router and a hinge template will form hinge mortises quickly and accurately. Once the router has been set up with the correct bit and adjusted to the right cutting depth, the template can be clamped on the door edge and a mortise machined in a matter of minutes. It will also mortise jambs. Most templates are adjustable for several common hinge sizes with either round or square corners. Templates are also available for routing mortises for lock faceplates and striker plates.

1 Mark the hinge locations

Leave the hinge leaf on the doorjamb. Set the door into place, using shims to wedge it exactly. Make sure the gaps at the bottom and the top of the door are even. With a pencil or a knife, mark the locations of the bottom and top of each hinge.

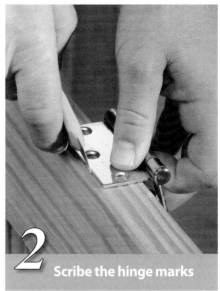

2 Scribe the hinge marks

Mark the outline of the hinges by holding the hinge in place as a template. Use a utility knife to make a light mark around each hinge. A handy tool called a butt marker has chisel edges that make indentations for a perfect cut. Hold it in place and tap it with a hammer.

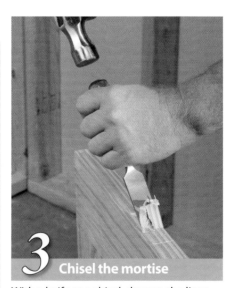

3 Chisel the mortise

With a knife or a chisel, deepen the lines marking the outside edges of the hinge until they are the full depth of the mortise. Holding the chisel with the beveled edge down, cut away enough material so that the hinge half sits flush with the surface of the door edge.

4 Install the hinge

Remove the pin from the hinge and install the separate halves on the door and jamb. Position a hinge half in its mortise and mark it for drilling with a center punch. Be careful to drill straight pilot holes so the screw heads sit flush. Drive screws into all the holes. Hang the door by aligning the hinge sections and reinserting the pin.

Installing a lockset

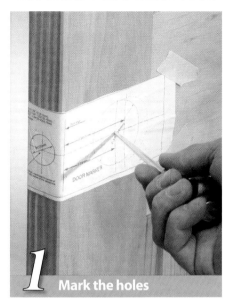

1 Mark the holes

Locksets or deadbolts come with paper or cardboard templates to help position them on the door. If a strike plate is already in the jamb, align the template with it so you won't have to cut a new mortise. If not, place the lock 36 inches from the floor. Tape or hold the template against the door, as shown. Pierce the template with an awl to mark the hole positions in the door face and edge.

2 Drill the holes

Bore the hole through the face of the door first, using a holesaw. To avoid splintering the door face, drill just until the pilot bit of the holesaw pokes through the other side. Then bore from the other side. Drill the edge with a spade bit; be sure to hold the bit parallel to the surface of the door and perpendicularly to its edge. Some locksets require that you continue drilling into the rear of the large hole another half inch.

3 Mortise the latch bolt

Insert the bolt through the smaller hole and hold it centered in the door while you mark for its mortise. Use a sharp pencil or a knife to mark the outline. Cut and chisel a mortise as you did for the hinges (opposite page). Depending on the type of bolt, the mortise may need to be deeper near the center than at the edges.

4 Install the bolt and handles

Install the bolt by setting it into the mortise, drilling pilot holes, and driving the screws provided. Install the lockset or handles according to the manufacturer's directions. Tighten all screws. Test the mechanisms to make sure they operate smoothly; you may need to clean out or widen your holes.

5 Install the strike plate

Mark the jamb for the correct location of the strike plate. The latch or bolt should be centered vertically in the strike opening and should enter the doorjamb. Mortise the jamb, drill pilot holes, and install the strike with the screws provided.

SELECT THE CORRECT DRILL BITS

Most lockset manufacturers call for a 2⅛-inch hole in the face of the door and a ⅞-inch hole in the door edge. But don't take that for granted; when you buy the handle or lockset, check the instructions and buy the right drill bits at the same time.

A standard holesaw works best for the large hole. An adjustable hole cutter works, but it is harder to use successfully to bore through a door. It cuts more slowly and may result in a rougher cut. But you can use it for different sizes of holes on other projects.

A spade bit works fine for the smaller hole, but if you want a more precise cut, use a Forstner bit.

Installing a deadbolt lock

- **TIME:** About 1 hour
- **SKILLS:** Drilling holes, mortising, assembling parts
- **TOOLS:** Drill with the required bits, chisel, knife

Deadbolt locks add security to doors. These locks have long bolts that reach into the jamb and sometimes into the framing.

A double-cylinder deadbolt, which locks with a key on the inside as well as the outside, offers the best security in situations where an intruder could reach through a broken or forced window to unlock the thumb turn on a single-cylinder deadbolt lock. However, it is not safe in case of fire—if you don't have the key handy, you could be stuck inside.

When purchasing a deadbolt, look for a bolt that extends 1 inch or more at full extension. This ensures a degree of strength against forced entry. The collar surrounding the bolt should be of substantial construction.

Install a strike plate with screws that go into the wall stud to give the bolt a stout seat.

FRENCH AND PATIO DOOR SECURITY RETROFITS

Although less secure than single doors, French and patio sliding doors need not be the weak points in your home security. Newer installations have two- and three-point locking systems that secure the doors at the top, bottom, and latch. However, you don't need to replace your old doors to gain added security for your home.

French doors that open inward can be fitted with sliding headbolts and footbolts or rack bolts top and bottom. A rack bolt is like a small deadbolt that is operated from the inside with a splined key. Turning the key several rotations extends the lock bolt into a hole in the doorjamb or sill. Rack bolts fit into holes bored into the door. Sliding bolts that mount on the surface of the door are somewhat easier to install.

If your French door opens outward, a secure latch and hinges with nonremovable pins enhance your security.

Fit sliding doors with a patio door bolt lock that attaches to the bottom of the fixed frame. These locks push through to the sliding door frame in the center and on the side frame. Drop-down security bars prevent the sliding panel from opening.

Rack bolts can be installed on sliding doors. However, they often are left unlocked, defeating the purpose.

High-strength plastic glazing and laminated safety glass are harder to break out than tempered glass.

1 Drill holes and cut mortise

Following the same techniques as for a lockset (see page 125), mark the position of the two holes and drill them, taking care to hold the drill perpendicularly to the door. Insert the bolt and latch face into their holes and mark for the mortise with a sharp knife. Cut the mortise with a chisel (see page 124).

2 Assemble the lock

Screw the latch face into the mortise. For many lock types, you'll need to use a screwdriver to partially extend the bolt. Insert the lock tailpiece through the slot in the bolt mechanism and slip on the interior thumb turn or lock until the two pieces sit against the door. Fasten the retaining screws. Install the strike plate.

Installing a prehung door

■ **TIME:** 2 hours to install a prehung unit in a rough opening

■ **SKILLS:** Nailing, leveling, shimming

■ **TOOLS:** Hammer, level, framing square, plumb bob, tape measure or ruler, saw or utility knife

A prehung door costs a little more than buying a door, doorjamb kit, and trim separately. But it saves you time and may result in a better installation. With a prehung door, you avoid having to cut the jamb, three stop pieces, and six casing pieces; mortise and install hinges; and drill and mortise for the handle and the strike plate.

Test-fit the prehung door unit in the rough opening. Check the hinge-side jamb for plumb and the jamb head for level. If the jamb head isn't level, raise whichever jamb side makes it level. Measure the distance between the bottom of the raised jamb side and the floor, then shorten the other jamb side by that amount.

Tack the hinge-side jamb into the rough opening. Attach a plumb bob to the top of the hinge-side jamb. Use a tape measure or ruler to measure the gap between the string and the jamb at several points, and plumb the jamb side. Slide overlapping pairs of shims into the gaps between the jamb and the rough opening at the top, bottom, and middle, and at each hinge location. Adjust the shim thickness to plumb the jamb side. Nail the jamb to the framing through the shims. Trim off the shim ends with a saw or utility knife so they are flush with the surface.

Shim and nail the head jamb to the header in the rough opening. The gap between the top of the door and the head jamb should be uniform from left to right and $1/8$ to $3/16$ inch wide, about the same as the space on the hinge side of the jamb.

Attach the latch-side jamb to the framing. The gap between the door and the jamb on the latch side should be about the same as the top and hinge-side gaps. Adjust by moving the jamb with your hand and inserting shims. Nail the jamb into place. Open and close the door to check that it clears the jamb by a consistent $1/8$ inch. Drive 8d finishing nails every 16 inches through the latch-side casing. Tack the door stops into position and check them by closing the door. Attach the stops.

Remove the center screw from the top hinge leaf and replace it with one long enough to penetrate into the framing. This helps prevent the door from sagging and binding.

Install the casing on both sides of the door. Mount the door hardware.

BEFORE YOU INSTALL

Make sure the door opens in the right direction and is the right size.

Test-fit the lockset in prebored holes. Holes that are too small can be redrilled. Holes that are too large will have to be plugged and rebored. It is easier to return a prehung door for a different one than to attempt to make a hole smaller. Another choice is to buy a lockset that fits the door.

Install a standard prehung door

Set the door into the opening and shim it, if necessary, to plumb it. Temporarily attach the hinge side of the jamb to the framing. Check the other two jamb pieces for square with a framing square and by closing the door; the gap should be even all around. Shim as necessary and attach all sides of the jamb. Install the casing.

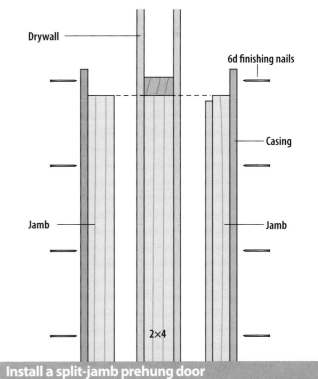

Drywall

6d finishing nails

Casing

Jamb

Jamb

2×4

Install a split-jamb prehung door

With this type of prehung door, the jamb is split, and the casing remains attached to the two jamb halves. Install the jamb half that has the door attached, just as you would a standard prehung door. Slip in the second half and cover the joint between the two with the stop molding provided.

Installing a window

■ **TIME:** 3 to 4 hours per window
■ **SKILLS:** Layout, measuring, cutting, and hammering
■ **TOOLS:** Hammer, reciprocating saw, caulking gun, circular saw, tape measure, level, drill

Before you buy a replacement for an old window, consider the window's location and whether you want a smaller or larger replacement. Or you might replace a sliding window with a double-hung. Don't assume that you must replace your old window with an exact duplicate.

SHOPPING TIPS

Look for the National Fenestration Rating Council (NFRC) label. It states that the window you purchased meets council standards.

The lower a window's U-value, the better its insulation factor. A U-value of 0.35 or below is recommended for cold climates. The window should have at least double glazing and low-E coating.

Where summertime heat is a concern, install windows with double glazing and spectrally selective coatings. These windows reduce heat gain.

Select windows with air leakage ratings of 0.3 cubic foot per minute or less.

Look for Energy Star and Energy Guide labels on the windows.

1 Prepare the opening

If your replacement window is not the same size as the original window, resize the rough opening. For a direct replacement window, follow the manufacturer's instructions for removing the old window and preparing the opening.

2 Test-fit the window

Have a helper assist you with placing the window into the center of the opening. Support the window with wooden blocks or shims.

3 Check for level

Make sure that the window is level and plumb. Adjust with shims and blocking.

4 Tack in place

If the window has nailing fins, drive 2-inch roofing nails through the holes. Leave the nailheads exposed so you can remove the nails if you encounter problems during the installation.

5 Check for plumb

If the window is square and the sill is level, the sides should be plumb. Check again for plumb. Adjust by placing shims between the window and framing. Open and close the window to make sure it operates smoothly. Fasten the window in place.

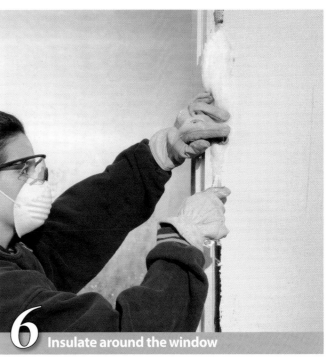

6 Insulate around the window

Insulation saves on heating bills by preventing outside air from entering. Push the insulation into the gap, but don't pack it tightly. Always wear gloves, protective eyewear, and a dust mask when handling fiberglass insulation.

7 Attach the exterior casing

Fasten the casing while checking the head jamb for level and the side jambs for plumb. Drive nails or screws on 12-inch centers. Caulk the gap between the window casing and the siding, as well as underneath the sill. Use a quality exterior caulk.

8 Finish the interior

Install interior trim. Full trimwork for a window includes the stool, apron, and window casing. Decide whether to install stain-grade or paint-grade trim. Attach the moldings and caulk the perimeter of the window.

Planning for new cabinets

■ **TIME:** 1 day to map out your space, 1 day to install cabinets for a medium-size kitchen

■ **SKILLS:** Precise measuring, leveling, drilling, driving screws

■ **TOOLS:** Level, tape measure, drill, pry bar, hammer

You can give old cabinets a new look by painting them and replacing the doors and hardware. Or you can hire a company that specializes in applying new finishes. Often, however, the best solution is to install new cabinets. With careful planning and modest carpentry skills, you can install new kitchen cabinets yourself.

When designing a kitchen, measure your space exactly and map out a wall plan on a piece of graph paper. As you plan, allow an extra inch or so for the width of the stove or refrigerator and for overhead clearance. Make sure that all cabinet doors, as well as those on the dishwasher and range, can open freely.

Many people prefer to have a soffit—a partial wall—coming down from the ceiling to meet the top of the wall cabinets. Building soffits is a lot of work; consider topping off wall cabinets with crown molding instead (see pages 114–116).

Unless you're a real stickler for symmetry, there's no reason to make the wall cabinets the same width as the base cabinets. Your cabinet supply center can help you design a new layout.

As you plan for new cabinets, upgrade the rest of your kitchen as well. An ideal time to add electrical outlets, undercabinet lights, or new flooring is after the old cabinets have been removed. Run new plumbing at this time if necessary. Patch and paint your walls too.

CHOOSING CABINETS

Most manufacturers have several lines of cabinets, each priced according to the quality of materials used in their construction. You can save money by buying unassembled or assembled but unfinished cabinets.

Closely inspect cabinets before buying. The doors should swing freely, latch securely, and line up straight. Drawers should glide on two metal tracks. Adjustable hinges are a plus because doors get out of alignment over time.

Particleboard and hardboard cabinets often come with hardwood or plastic veneers; once scratched, these are difficult to repair. Screws driven into particleboard do not hold well, and hinges can come loose.

Although more expensive, hardwood is the best choice for doors, frames, and sides. It holds up against abuse and can be repaired. When finished properly, hardwood is easy to maintain.

WALL CABINETS

12", 15", or 18" units for installation above stove or refrigerator

Wall filler   Corner filler

30" or 42" wall cabinets

BASE CABINETS

$34\frac{1}{2}$"-high base

Sink base for a double sink

Cabinet to store baking sheets and trays

Base fillers

Corner cabinet with revolving shelves

Select from many cabinet types

Ready-made cabinets come in standard sizes that vary in 3-inch increments, so you probably need to buy filler pieces to make up gaps of 1 to 3 inches. Typically base cabinets are 24 inches deep and $34\frac{1}{2}$ inches tall; once you add the countertop, the surface is 36 inches high. Wall cabinets usually are 12 inches deep and 30 or 42 inches tall; some are shorter to fit above stoves, refrigerators, and other appliances. Allow space if you plan to install an over-the-stove microwave. Special base cabinets are available for corners or for sinks.

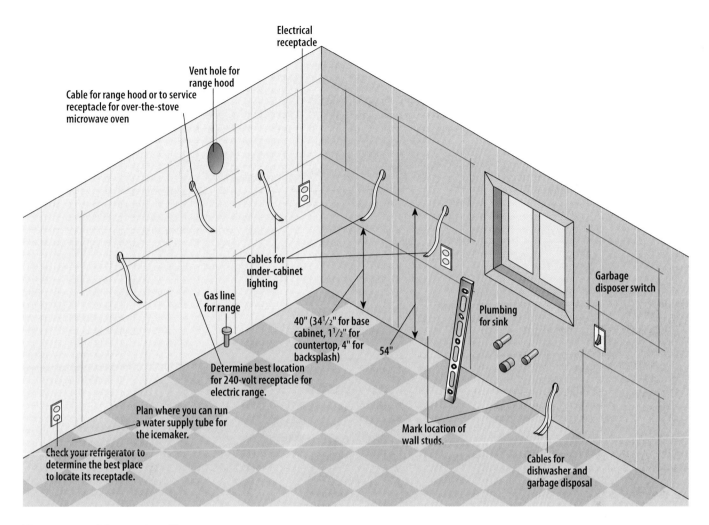

Electrical receptacle

Vent hole for range hood

Cable for range hood or to service receptacle for over-the-stove microwave oven

Cables for under-cabinet lighting

Gas line for range

Determine best location for 240-volt receptacle for electric range.

Plan where you can run a water supply tube for the icemaker.

Check your refrigerator to determine the best place to locate its receptacle.

40" (34½" for base cabinet, 1½" for countertop, 4" for backsplash)

54"

Mark location of wall studs.

Plumbing for sink

Garbage disposer switch

Cables for dishwasher and garbage disposal

Prepare and lay out walls

Remove the old cabinets. Check your floor for level. If it's off by half an inch or less, you can shim the base cabinets. If it's far out of level, consider leveling the floor before installing new cabinets. Placing the cabinets over an uneven floor can lead to door and drawer problems. If installing new flooring, it is easiest to do before you install cabinets. Also check your walls for plumb. Depending on which way they lean, you may need to move the cabinets or plan on shimming them plumb.

Start at the highest point of the floor (see page 132) and draw outlines of your base cabinets on the wall. Measure 19½ inches up from the cabinet tops (to allow for the thickness of the countertop) and draw outlines of your wall cabinets. The standard kitchen countertop height is 36 inches; the bottom of the wall cabinets should be 54 inches above the floor.

Look at your outlines and visualize how your kitchen is to look and work. Use old cabinets or pieces of wood of the same dimensions to get a clear idea of how the cabinets fit into the space. Now, rather than later, is the best time to change your mind about the cabinet layout you want. You may find it better to leave more room around a window or give yourself a couple more inches of traffic space. Be sure that all doors— entry, appliance, and cabinet—have room to open.

Rough in the plumbing and complete the electrical work before installing cabinets. Estimate the wattage demand of your lighting and appliances and plan your electrical circuits to prevent overloading.

Decide where you want electrical receptacles. Be sure to account for the height of the backsplash (4 inches) as well as the countertop when

locating outlets. Ground fault circuit interrupters (GFCIs) are required for all receptacles within 6 feet of a sink. Run wiring for the dishwasher and garbage disposer as well as switches for lights and the garbage disposer.

Plan for undercabinet lighting. To install fluorescent fixtures under the cabinets, run cable as shown above. Where you poke the cables through the wall depends on how your cabinets are constructed. You also can install low-voltage halogen lighting after the cabinets are installed.

Buy the range hood and find out where the exhaust hole should go in your wall. Cut the hole and install the necessary ductwork.

Patch the portions of the walls that show after the cabinets are installed and paint them or hang wallpaper. Make light pencil marks on the walls showing the location of your studs.

Installing base cabinets

- **TIME:** 4 to 6 hours for a medium-size kitchen
- **SKILLS:** Leveling and plumbing, drilling and driving screws, shimming, clamping
- **TOOLS:** Tape measure; level; stud finder; hammer; drill with bit set, driver bit, and counterbore bit; nail set; jigsaw with wood-cutting blade; pry bar; clamps, chalkline

Find the highest point of your floor by using a straight 2×4. Start the layout at that point; you can shim cabinets up but not down. Measure up 34½ inches from the high point and snap a level chalkline to show where the tops of the cabinets go. As you work, take care not to damage the cabinets with your tools. Use screws (often supplied by the manufacturer), never nails.

If a baseboard or other piece of molding is in the way, remove it and cut it; don't cut the cabinet to fit around the molding.

If you are installing wall cabinets above the base cabinets, install the wall cabinets first. It is easier without the lower ones in the way. But watch your head as you install the base cabinets.

Base cabinets must be anchored to studs in the kitchen walls. Use a stud finder to determine where the studs are located in the walls. Generally studs are spaced 16 or sometimes 24 inches apart, so after you find the first one, measure to find another one and verify the spacing with the stud finder. Mark both edges of each stud.

PLAN FOR THE FUTURE

The cabinets and countertops you install will be in your home for a long time. It pays to buy durable, well-made cabinetry that will stand up to years of use.

Beware of design fads or kitchen styles that may not fit the way you live and cook. Over time they can become annoyances. You may want to consider resale value too; a well-planned, functional kitchen always is a selling point for your house. Look at a lot of kitchen ideas and designs and picture yourself using those kitchens. Pick the best ideas to incorporate into your plan. Think about your plan, and look at it critically for a few days before you begin the project.

1 Check for level

Starting at the highest point of the floor, set the first cabinet into place. Check that the cabinet is level from front to back as well as from side to side. Double-check the framing to make certain it is plumb. Shim the bottom of the cabinet if necessary and recheck that the cabinet is level.

Measure the height of the cabinet. This dimension should be about 34½ inches. Snap a chalkline on the wall along the top of this cabinet to indicate the top edge of the new cabinets. Attach cleats to the floor for the cabinet.

2 Install the corner cabinet first

Install the first cabinet in a corner, if possible. Shim the cabinet to position the top level with the line on the wall. Make sure the cabinet is level in all directions. Shim if necessary.

3 Attach the cabinet to the wall

Drill pilot holes and drive in screws through the cabinet framing (not the thin plywood backing) and into wall studs. Wherever the framing is not tight against the wall, use shims to keep the cabinet plumb. Recheck the cabinet for level in both directions before moving on to the next unit. Use a saw or chisel to cut off any protruding shims.

4 Join cabinets together

To ensure tight, even joints between the cabinets, clamp them in place before fastening. Make sure they are flush with each other, not only along their faces but also at the top. Drill pilot holes for countersunk screws (see page 33), then drive in screws to hold the units together firmly. Attach the cabinet to the wall as you did the first one.

5 Install toe-kick or base

If you have to shim the cabinets, an unsightly gap between the base and the floor may appear. If the toe-kick was preinstalled, remove it by gently prying it off. Reinstall it flush with the floor. A slight gap along the top of the toe-kick doesn't show. If the toe-kick was not preinstalled, simply nail it flush with the floor. To dress up the toe-kick, you can put a cove base over it.

HELPFUL TIPS FROM THE PROS

- Think through the process before starting. Draw the cabinet layout to scale for reference throughout the installation process.
- Most stock cabinets are available in 3-inch increments, beginning as narrow as 9 inches. Map out your cabinets on graph paper before purchasing and installing. Maximize space and minimize filler strips by making slight modifications—within the standard increments—to the widths of your new cabinets.
- Even when you plan to install cabinets yourself, consider hiring a kitchen planner to assist you in planning, designing, and measuring your new cabinets and other kitchen components. If you do not want to hire a designer, find out whether the home center or cabinet dealer offers measuring services. Precise measurements are essential.
- Be careful when removing old cabinets. Do as little damage as possible to the walls and ceiling.

Installing wall cabinets

- **TIME:** 2 to 3 hours for a group of six standard cabinets
- **SKILLS:** Leveling, drilling, driving screws, shimming
- **TOOLS:** Tape measure, level, ruler, drill, bit set, chalkline, utility knife, framing square, wood shims, hammer, nail set, clamps, screwdriver bit

It's easier to install wall cabinets before base cabinets because you have more room to work and lift the cabinets into position. If you do install the base cabinets first, protect them with drop cloths or cardboard while working on the wall cabinets. If you are installing undercabinet lighting, you may need to drill holes in the wall cabinets for the cable, depending on how the cabinets are constructed.

Cabinets are constructed square and straight. Unfortunately, the same is not always true of kitchen walls. Walls that are not plumb can affect the fit of your cabinets; check for plumb before

beginning. Have an abundant supply of shims handy. When properly placed, shims can plumb and level a cabinet despite the irregularity of the wall on which it is mounted.

Also check that the wall is flat. A hump or dip in the wall racks and twists the cabinet, making the installation look wavy. Check the wall with a straight 2×4 as you did the floor (see page 132). Use shims and blocking to true the cabinets as you hang them.

Install the plumbing and electrical wiring for appliances before installing cabinets. Install electrical receptacles every 4 feet above the countertop along

the backsplash. Rough in cabinet lights and wall-mounted switches. Also mark the locations of all appliances, including the vent hood.

Start the installation in a corner and secure cabinets to the wall with screws driven through cabinet framing into wall studs. Where one side misses a stud, use toggle bolts or other fasteners recommended by the cabinet manufacturer. Do not hang cabinets with nails. Always enlist a helper when installing wall cabinets.

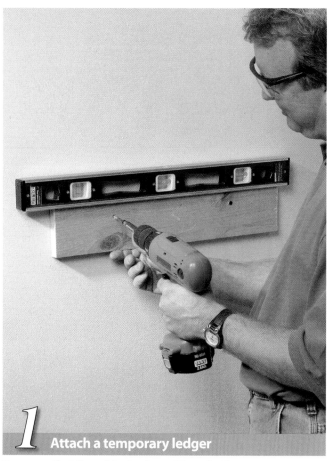

1 Attach a temporary ledger

To ensure that the cabinets align with each other, create a reference line. Use a level to mark a point 54 inches above the highest point on the floor. Snap a chalkline at this mark. Secure a straight board with its top edge along the line, which is where the bottom of your cabinets will be (18 inches above the countertop). Or you can make a 2×4 support of the appropriate height and rest the cabinets on top of it until they are fastened to the wall.

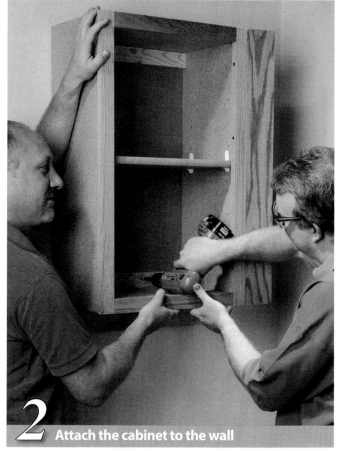

2 Attach the cabinet to the wall

If the cabinet is heavy, remove shelves and doors to make it manageable. With a helper or two, hold the first cabinet in place. It should rest on top of the guide. Check it for level and plumb. Slip in shims as necessary and drive screws through the top and bottom framing pieces into wall studs. For screw heads that remain visible, use finish washers. Some manufacturers supply plastic screw-head covers.

3 Install a spacer at a corner

Spacer

In most situations, join wall cabinets together as with base cabinets (see page 133). Spacers can be disguised easily in corners. Begin by attaching the spacer to the cabinet. Rip the spacer to the correct width, clamp it in place, drill and countersink pilot holes, and drive in three screws. Remove the clamps.

4 Fasten the next cabinet

Spacer

It usually is best not to cover any part of a cabinet frame, or you will have trouble closing cabinet doors. In corners, attach the cabinets by drilling and countersinking pilot holes through the spacer. Drive in screws through the spacer and into the frame of the next cabinet.

Attach a decorative valance above the sink. Clamp it in place to the edge of the cabinet. Drill counterbored pilot holes through the cabinet frame into the valance. Fasten with screws.

Using a utility knife, cut all exposed shims flush with the cabinets. Remove the temporary ledger when installation is complete. Trim molding is the perfect way to cover any gaps between the cabinets and walls. Finish by filling holes and sanding. Paint or stain to match the cabinets.

Install the cabinet doors. Check the doors for level and plumb. It may be necessary to adjust the hinges.

MORE HELPFUL PRO TIPS

- If you have a tall cabinet such as a pantry or a built-in oven, use it to determine the height of wall cabinets.
- Allow four to six weeks for cabinet delivery. Don't tear out existing cabinets until you know your new cabinets have arrived. Countertops generally take three to four weeks for delivery. Order countertops when you order the cabinets.
- Have a plumber and an electrician lined up to rough in new plumbing and electric right after you remove the old cabinets. Plan to have the plumber and electrician return right after you install the countertop.
- If your floors are not level, install base cabinets from the high side of the floor first and work your way to the low side. Shim the cabinets to level as you work. This prevents you from having to cut the underside of any cabinets.
- Use wood clamps to hold cabinets together while you predrill holes through the stiles.

CAUTION

SECURE CABINETS TO STUDS

All that holds wall cabinets up are screws driven into the wall. Stacks of plates and canned goods can add up to some extra-heavy loads, so make sure every cabinet is securely anchored to the wall. Fasteners driven into drywall or plaster alone do not do the job. Screws should go at least 1 inch into wall studs to safely support fully loaded cabinets.

Installing ceiling-hung cabinets

- **TIME:** 2 to 3 hours for a group of six standard cabinets
- **SKILLS:** Leveling, drilling, driving screws, shimming
- **TOOLS:** Tape measure, level, ruler, drill, bit set, chalkline, utility knife, framing square, wood shims, hammer, nail set, clamps, screwdriver bit

Most people say the kitchen and living room are their favorite places in their home. The idea of the great-room grew from combining these two favorite rooms. Open space is nice, but there's value in maintaining distinct areas for relaxing and cooking. A divider or buffer may be just the solution. Peninsula and ceiling-hung cabinets fill this need. They separate, yet don't isolate, while providing additional work surface and storage.

Adding ceiling cabinets

Mounting cabinets to the ceiling for an island or peninsula adds more storage space, as well as an area that brings the kitchen into adjoining rooms, creating a connection between spaces. You need to add blocking to support the cabinets.

1 Set the blocking

Determine the location of the cabinets. Following the manufacturer's specifications, measure the location of the blocking and attach it to the ceiling joists. If the joists run parallel to the cabinets, add 2×4s between the joists to hold the blocking.

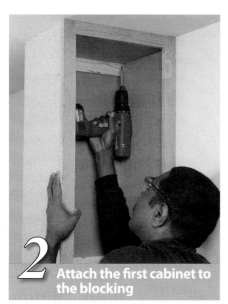

2 Attach the first cabinet to the blocking

Position the cabinet and drive screws into the blocking to secure the cabinet.

3 Level the next cabinet

Have a helper assist by holding the next cabinet in place. Make sure that the cabinet is plumb and level; otherwise the door will not shut properly. Few things are as annoying as a cabinet that pops open after you close it.

4 Fasten the cabinet

It usually is best not to cover any part of a cabinet frame or you will have trouble closing cabinet doors. In corners, attach the cabinets by drilling and countersinking pilot holes through a spacer. Drive screws through the spacer into the frame of the next cabinet.

Countertop ideas

Laminate countertops have evolved in durability and design. Unless you want a retro look with metal edging, self edging has replaced the metal strips, and durability has substantially improved. For added elegance you can incorporate wood and other laminate colors or textures into edging. Laminate countertops can provide the beauty and durability of more expensive materials at a fraction of the cost.

Neutral top fits any design
The neutral color of this laminate countertop works well with the natural tones throughout the kitchen. Laminate is strong and easy to clean, but it can chip. Care should be taken during installation and use.

Almost endless variety
Laminate countertops are available in myriad patterns, colors, and textures, making them versatile and affordable choices. This laminate bathroom countertop resembles natural wood. Stone-look laminate finishes also are popular.

ALTERNATIVE COUNTERTOP MATERIALS

Solid granite countertops are expensive, but they look great and last forever. Artificial solid-surface countertops, such as Corian and Avonite, also are extremely durable and come in a wide choice of colors and patterns. In most cases granite or composite tops should be fabricated and installed by professionals.

If you have tiling experience, you can cover a countertop with ceramic or granite tile. Begin with a solid, level plywood or backerboard base. Set ceramic tiles with tile adhesive or thinset mortar. Set granite tiles with silicone caulk. Your tile dealer can supply you with cutters, adhesives, and grout for both types of materials.

Installing a countertop

■ **TIME:** 2 to 3 hours to scribe and install a medium-size top

■ **SKILLS:** Precise measuring and cutting, scribing, fastening

■ **TOOLS:** Circular saw or jigsaw, belt sander, wrenches, router, iron, drill

Countertops covered with plastic laminate are durable and economical; thus, they are the most common choice. If your layout is straightforward, you can buy a ready-made, postformed top that has a curved front lip and an integrated backsplash. Factory-cut miters make corners easy to handle. Or you can build and laminate a square-edge top with separate backsplash. Analyze the situation carefully. If your walls are more than ³⁄₈ inch out of square or the layout is complex, you may need to consult a countertop professional.

1 Cut the top

To make a sink cutout, mark the top according to manufacturer's directions; usually the hole should be 1 inch smaller than the outside dimensions of the sink. Use a jigsaw with a fine-tooth, downcut blade. To cut a ready-made top to length, turn it upside down and use a circular saw with a straightedge guide. Support the scrap carefully or the laminate will crack.

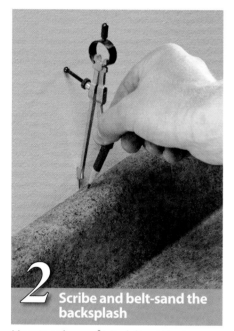

2 Scribe and belt-sand the backsplash

Most tops have a ³⁄₈-inch lip at the top of the backsplash that you can cut to accommodate wavy or out-of-square walls. Set the top into place against the wall and scribe the wall contour on the backsplash by running a compass along the wall. Don't try to cut off excess material; it will crack. Instead use a belt sander to carefully remove the material.

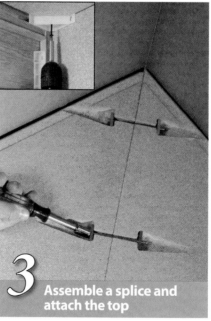

3 Assemble a splice and attach the top

Butt the pieces together on top of the base cabinets. Working from underneath, tighten the supplied bolts. Check the top as you work to make sure the splice is flat and the ends are even. To fasten the top into place (inset), drive screws up through the cabinet framing. Screws should be long enough to hold the top but not so long as to pierce the surface.

4 Attach end caps

For each exposed edge, buy an end cap (either left-hand or right-hand). To attach the end cap, warm it in the oven or use a household iron to melt the glue as you press it into place. Make sure all countertop edges are covered. After the cap is cool, use a router with a flush-trimming bit, or a file, to remove the excess material and form a uniform edge.

Glossary

For words not listed here, or for more information about those that are, refer to the index (pages 141–143).

Actual dimension. True size of a piece of lumber, after milling and drying. See nominal dimension.

Awl. A sharp-pointed tool used for making small starter holes for screws or for scribing lines.

Batt. A section of fiberglass insulation measuring 15 or 23 inches wide by 4 to 8 feet long.

Bevel cut. A rip cut or crosscut made at an angle through the thickness of a piece of wood.

Biscuit joiner. A mechanized tool used to cut incisions into lumber. Oval-shaped wooden biscuits are inserted into the incisions and glued to reinforce a joint.

Board. A piece of lumber that is less than 2 inches thick and more than 3 inches wide.

Board foot. The standard unit of measurement for wood. One board foot is equal to a piece 12×12×1 inches (nominal size).

Building codes. Community ordinances governing the manner in which a home or other structure may be constructed or modified. Most codes deal primarily with fire and health concerns and have separate sections relating to electrical, plumbing, and structural work.

Butt joint. A joint formed by two pieces of material when fastened end to end, end to face, or end to edge.

Casing. Molding around a door, window, or other opening.

Chamfer. A bevel cut made along the length of a board edge.

Cleat. A board attached to strengthen or add support to a structure.

Clinch. To hammer the exposed tip of a nail at an angle, bending its point into the wood for added joint strength.

Coped cut. A cut in the face of a piece of molding that follows the molding profile so the molding can butt against another piece at an inside corner.

Counterbore. To drive a screw below the surface of the surrounding wood. The void created is filled later with putty or a wooden plug.

Countersink. To drive in the head of a nail or screw so its top is flush with the surface of the surrounding wood.

Crosscut. To saw a piece of lumber across the grain.

Dado joint. A joint formed when the end of one member fits into a groove cut partway through the face of another member.

Dimensional lumber. A piece of lumber with nominal thickness of 2 inches that is at least 2 inches wide, used for framing.

Dowel. A piece of small-diameter wood rod used to reinforce joints.

Edging. Strips of wood or veneer used to cover the edges of plywood or boards.

End grain. The ends of wood fibers that are exposed at the ends of boards.

Filler. A pastelike compound used to hide surface imperfections in wood. One type, pore filler, levels the surface of wood that has a coarse grain.

Fire blocking. Short horizontal members sometimes nailed between framing studs, usually about halfway up the wall. They serve to slow a fire from moving up the framing space.

Flush. On the same plane as or level with a surrounding surface.

Furring. Lightweight strips of wood applied to walls to provide a plumb nailing surface for paneling or drywall.

Grain. The direction of fibers in a piece of wood; also refers to the pattern of the fibers.

Gusset. A piece of wood or plywood nailed or screwed over a joint to give it added strength.

Hardwood. Lumber derived from deciduous trees such as oaks, maples, and walnuts.

Header. The framing component spanning a door or window opening in a wall. A header supports the weight above it and serves as a nailing surface for the door or window frame.

Inside corner. The point at which two walls form an internal angle, as in the corner of a room.

Jamb. The top and side frames of a door or window opening.

Joists. Horizontal framing members that support a floor and/or ceiling.

Kerf. The void created when the blade of a saw removes material when it is cutting.

Lag screw. A screw, usually ¼ inch in diameter or larger, with a hexagonal head that can be screwed in with an adjustable or socket wrench.

Lap joint. The joint formed when one member overlaps another.

Ledger. A horizontal strip (typically lumber) used to provide support for the ends or edges of other members.

Level. The condition that exists when a surface is at true horizontal. Also a tool used to determine level.

Linear foot. Refers to the length of a board or piece of molding, in contrast to a board foot.

Miter joint. The joint formed when two members meet that have been cut at the same angle, usually 45 degrees.

Molding. A strip of wood, usually small-dimensioned, used to cover exposed edges or as a decoration.

Mortise. A shallow cutout in a board, usually used to recess hardware such as hinges. Deeper mortises receive tenons to make a joint.

Nominal dimension. The stated size of a piece of lumber such as 2×4 or 1×12. The actual dimension is somewhat smaller.

On center (OC). Designates the distance from the center of one regularly spaced framing member to the center of the next one.

Outside corner. The point at which two walls form an external angle; the corner you usually can walk around.

Particleboard. Panels made from compressed wood particles and glue.

Pilot hole. A small hole drilled into a wooden member to avoid splitting the wood when driving in a screw or nail.

Plumb. The condition that exists when a member is at true vertical.

Pressure-treated wood. Lumber and sheet goods impregnated with one of several solutions to make the wood more impervious to rot.

Rabbet. A step-shape cut made along the edge of a piece of wood; used to join boards tightly.

Rip. To saw lumber or sheet goods parallel to its grain.

Roughing in. The framing stage of a carpentry project. Framing later is concealed in the finishing stages.

Rout. To shape edges or cut grooves using a router.

Sealer. A protective, usually clear coating applied to wood or metal.

Setting nails. Driving in the heads of nails slightly below the surface of the wood using a nail set.

Shim. A thin strip or wedge of wood or other material used to fill a gap between two adjoining components or to help establish level or plumb.

Soffit. Covering attached between wall cabinets and the ceiling.

Softwood. Lumber derived from coniferous trees such as pines, firs, cedars, or redwoods.

Square. The condition that exists when one surface is at a 90-degree angle to another. Also a tool used to determine when surfaces are square.

Studs. Vertical wood or metal framing members spaced at regular intervals within a wall.

Taper. A gradual and uniform decrease in the width or thickness of a board.

Taping. The process of covering drywall joints with paper tape and joint compound to smooth them.

Three-four-five method. A way to check corners for square. Measure 3 feet along one side and 4 feet along the other. If the corner is square, the diagonal distance between the two points equals 5 feet.

Toenail. To drive a nail at an angle to hold together two pieces of material, usually studs and a plate in a wall.

Tongue-and-groove joint. A joint made by fitting the projecting tongue on one member into a corresponding groove on the other member.

Top plate. The topmost horizontal element of a stud-frame wall.

Vapor barrier. A waterproof membrane in a floor, wall, or ceiling that blocks the transfer of condensation to the inner surface.

Veneer. A thin layer of wood, often a decorative wood laminated to the surface of a more common wood.

Warp. Any of several lumber defects caused by uneven shrinkage of wood cells.

Index

A

Adhesives, 44, 51–52, 95, 98
Antiquing, 58
Awls, 32, 37

B

Base cabinets, installing, 132–133
Base molding, 111–113
Basement
    furring walls, 66–67
    moisture damage, 69
Bedroom closet, organizing, 108–109
Belt sander, 54, 55, 80
Beveled rip cut, 29
Biscuit joiner, 50, 80
Bits
    drill, 31–34
    router, 30
Bolts
    fastening with, 39
    selecting, 95
Brackets, 96, 104
Building codes, 8
Butt joint, 45, 50

C

Cabinets
    choosing, 130
    hanging, 104–105
    hardware, 97
    installing base cabinets, 132–133
    installing ceiling-hung cabinets, 136
    installing wall cabinets, 134–135
    planning for new, 130–131
Carriage bolt, 39, 95
Carrying materials, 93
Caulking, 44
Ceiling-hung cabinets, installing, 136
Ceramic tile, drilling through, 34
Chair rail, 120–121
Chalkline, 118, 121
Chisels, 25–26
Circles, marking, 17
Circular saw, 18–20, 79
Clamping techniques, 42–43
Closet, organizing bedroom, 108–109

Clothing measurements, 108
Combination square, 13, 15
Compass, 16–17
Concrete, drilling through, 34
Coping, 114–115
Coping saw, 24, 115
Corners
    framing, 63
    squaring, 14
Countertops
    design ideas, 137
    installing, 138
    materials, 137
Crosscut, 22, 27, 29
Crown molding, 114–116
Curves, cutting with jigsaw, 24
Cutting techniques
    circular saw, 18–20
    drywall, 68–69
    handsaw, 22
    inside and contour cuts, 23–24
    laminate, 51
    mitering, 20–21
    plunge cut, 20
    radial arm saw, 29
    table saw, 27–28

D

Dado, 26, 28, 29, 46, 47–48, 102
Deadbolt lock, installing, 126
Detail sander, 55
Dividers, 17
Door
    cutting, 123
    deadbolt lock installation, 126
    French and patio, 126
    hinge installation, 124
    lockset installation, 125
    prehung, installing, 127
    repairing problems, 122–123
    roughing in an opening, 74
Dowels, 49
Drills and drilling, 31–34, 79.80
Drywall

cutting, 23, 68–69
finishing tips, 72
hanging, 70–71
laying out, 68–69
taping, 72–73
Drywall square, 14, 68

F

Filling, 57, 113, 119
Finishes, 58
Framing
    corners, 63
    metal, 64–65
    roughing in an opening, 74
    walls, 60–63
Framing square, 13
Furring basement walls, 66–67

G

Glue, 98
Gluing techniques, 42–43
Grinder, 80
Guide, saw, 19, 20

H

Half-lap joint, 47–48
Handsaw, 22, 77
Hardware
    selecting, 96–97
    shelf, 96, 104
Hinges
    installing door, 124
    types, 96–97
Holesaw, 32, 125

I

I-beam, framing around, 74

J

Jigsaw, 23–24, 79
Joint
    biscuit, 50
    butt, 45, 50
    dado, 26, 28, 29, 46, 47–48, 102
    dowel, 49
    edge-to-edge, 50
    half-lap, 47–48

Index *(continued)*

hardware reinforcement, 96
lap, 46
miter, 46
scarf, 111, 112
T, 50

K
Kerf, 11
Keyhole saw, 23
Kickback, 18

L
Laminate, 51–52
Lap joint, 46
Level, checking for, 14–15
Levels, 14–15
Lockset, installing, 125
Lumber, 84–85. *See also* Wood

M
Machine bolt, 39, 95
Marking techniques, 10–11, 16–17
Masonry, drilling through, 34
Masonry nails, 36
Measuring
    mistakes, 12
    in place, 12
    techniques, 10–11
Metal
    drilling through, 34
    fastening with screws, 38
    studs, 64–65
Miter cuts, 20–21
Miter joint, 46
Mitersaw, 21, 80
Molding
    building decorative shelves, 106–107
    buying, 111
    chair rail, 120–121
    design ideas, 110
    installing base molding, 111–113
    installing crown molding, 114–116
    plastic, 90, 116

selecting, 90–91
wall frames, 117–119
Mortise, 25–26, 124, 125

N
Nailer, 116
Nailing drywall, 70
Nailing techniques, 35–36
Nails
    cutting, 40
    masonry, 36
    removing, 40–41
    selecting, 94
    size, 35, 94
Nut, cutting, 41

O
Orbital sander, 80
Organizing
    bedroom closet, 108–109
    tools, 82–83

P
Painting, 58
Pilot hole, 33, 36, 37, 95, 98, 113
Pipe, framing around, 74
Planing, 53–54, 122
Plumb
    cabinets, 15
    checking for, 14
Plunge cut, 20
Power hammer, 67
Projects, 99–138

R
Rabbet, 28, 29
Radial arm saw, 27, 29, 81
Reciprocating saw, 81
Rip cuts
    beveled, 28
    marking for, 11
    with radial arm saw, 29
    with tablesaw, 27, 28
Roughing in an opening, 74
Routers and routering, 30, 81, 124

S
Safety
    adhesives, 52
    metal studs, 64
    mitersaw, 21
    radial arm saw, 29
    sanding, 55
    tablesaw, 27
    tool tips, 8, 81
Sanding, 55–56
Saws
    blade depth, setting, 19
    circular, 18–20, 79
    coping, 24, 115
    handsaw, 22, 77
    holesaw, 32, 125
    jigsaw, 23–24, 79
    keyhole, 23
    miter, 21, 27, 29, 80
    radial arm, 27, 29, 81
    reciprocating, 81
    table, 27–28, 81
Scarf joint, 111, 112
Screws
    fastening with, 37–38
    hanging drywall with, 70
    pilot hole and counterbore sizes, 98
    removing, 40–41
    selecting, 95
Scribing, 53
Shaping, 53–54
Sheet goods, selecting, 92
Shelves
    building, 102–103
    decorative molding, 106–107
    hanging, 104–105
    layout, 104
    spans, 104
Shims, 15, 61, 122, 123, 127
Shoe molding, 113
Soundproofing walls, 62
Squares, 13–14
Storing materials, 93

Studs
    length, 60
    metal, 64–65

T

T-bevel, 16

T-joint, 50

Tablesaw, 27–28, 81

Taping drywall, 72–73

Techniques, carpentry, 9–58

Templates, 16

Tenon, 28

Terminology, 6

Toenailing, 63

Tools. *See also specific tools*
    hand, 76–78
    organizing, 82–83
    power, 79–81
    safety tips, 8, 81
    sharpening, 25–26

Triangular layout square, 13

W

Wall cabinets, installing, 134–135

Wall frames, 117–119

Walls
    building in place, 62–63
    building techniques, 60–61
    furring basement, 66–67
    soundproofing, 62

Water level, 15

Window installation, 128–129

Wood
    grades, 84
    inspecting, 84
    lumber selection, 84–85
    selecting, 86–89

Workbench, building, 100–101

METRIC CONVERSIONS

U.S. Units to Metric Equivalents			Metric Units to U.S. Equivalents		
To convert from	**Multiply by**	**To get**	**To convert from**	**Multiply by**	**To get**
Inches	25.4	Millimeters	Millimeters	0.0394	Inches
Inches	2.54	Centimeters	Centimeters	0.3937	Inches
Feet	30.48	Centimeters	Centimeters	0.0328	Feet
Feet	0.3048	Meters	Meters	3.2808	Feet
Yards	0.9144	Meters	Meters	1.0936	Yards
Square inches	6.4516	Square centimeters	Square centimeters	0.1550	Square inches
Square feet	0.0929	Square meters	Square meters	10.764	Square feet
Cubic inches	16.387	Cubic centimeters	Cubic centimeters	0.0610	Cubic inches
Cubic feet	0.0283	Cubic meters	Cubic meters	35.315	Cubic feet
Cubic feet	28.316	Liters	Liters	0.0353	Cubic feet

To convert from degrees Fahrenheit (F) to degrees Celsius (C), first subtract 32, then multiply by $5/9$.

To convert from degrees Celsius to degrees Fahrenheit, multiply by $9/5$, then add 32.

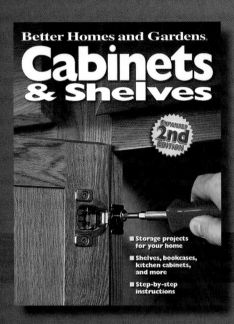
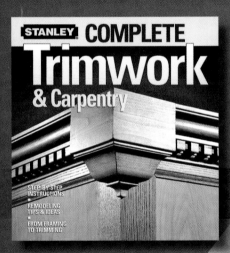
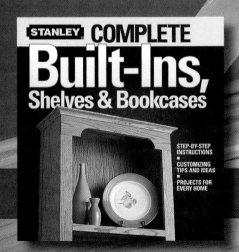